Faces
of **Stradey**
Park

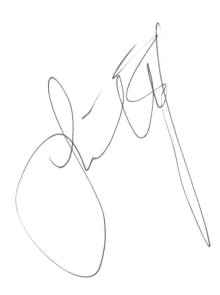

First published in Great Britain in 2008
by Bryngold Books Ltd.,
Golden Oaks, 98 Brynau Wood, Cimla,
Neath, South Wales, SA11 3YQ.
www.bryngoldbooks.com

Typesetting, layout, editing and design
by Bryngold Books

ISBN 978-1-905900-09-1

Printed in Wales
by Gomer Press,
Llandysul, Ceredigion.

Faces of Stradey Park

Words **Andy Pearson**
Pictures **Terry Morris**

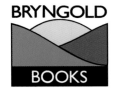

BRYNGOLD
BOOKS

SCARLETS

Faces of Stradey Park has been
produced in association with

Contents

Memories are

WHEN the emotion was stripped away there was little to imply a gladiatorial arena of blood, sweat and tears.

As bureaucracy plodded through 2006 and 2007 it did so with no hint of fleet-footed heroics, muscular archenemies and the crunch of body on body. There was no salute to eager crowds of many-a-thousand; no acknowledgment that, for almost 130 years, Llanelli's finest rugby players had done battle at Stradey Park.

A report to members of Carmarthenshire Council in summer 2006 explained simply that Stradey Park was located to the north of the A484 Sandy Road in the Sandy Park area on the west side of Llanelli town centre. Officers said: "The site is generally surrounded by housing and takes its access through residential streets. It is generally level with the rugby stadium at its heart.

"The main and signposted entrance to the rugby ground is gained via Maes-y-Coed from the A484. A secondary entrance is gained from Stradey Park Avenue which leads due east to a junction with New Road."

Councillors heard that there were eight bus routes passing close to the site, with destinations including Swansea, Carmarthen, Gorseinon, Kidwelly, Burry Port and Tesco at Parc Trostre. A cycleway followed a disused rail track that ran northwards close to the eastern boundary of the site. The report intoned: "The Stradey Park land comprises the stadium, club offices and a social club, training pitches, a car park and an area of waste ground.

"The stadium comprises four stands, three of which - the north, south and west - are of steel and concrete construction while the eastern stand consists of an earth bank with concrete steps forming terracing for spectators.

"There are rugby training pitches to the west of the stadium. To the east is an area of grassed waste ground used for car parking on matchdays.

"South of the stadium is a Tarmaced car park and, adjoining the car park, is a single-storey brick building which houses offices, a bar and social club. High voltage power cables run north-to-south over the eastern area of waste ground."

Directly to the south, councillors were told, was an area mainly covered in hard standing, with three derelict steel and concrete buildings together with two fuel pumps.

The report continued: "The land immediately to the north is occupied by a cricket ground, several tennis courts and rugby pitches and associated buildings beyond which - on land rising slightly

made of this

towards residential properties in St Margaret's Drive before Stradey Road - are open fields and woodland.

"Land to the west, east and south of Stradey Park is predominantly residential, comprising a mixture of terraced and semi-detached properties."

An accompanying list of planning approvals dating back to the time when Phil Bennett led the British Lions to New Zealand only whispered about the stadium's remarkable social history.

This list included:

Sept 1977 Replacement of floodlighting towers

July 1978 Changing rooms, stores, showers and toilets

July 1985 Sponsors lounge extension

Dec 2002 Replacement of floodlight mast with 35m mast and the installation of high level telecommunications equipment and ground level cabin.

Other work had included the demolition of the famous Tanner Bank in 1990. In its place rose the £400,000 North Stand and Enclosure.

By the time the 1991 Rugby World Cup game between Australia and Argentina was played there, the year 1879 seemed a world away. Yet that's when members of the then-named Llanelly Football Club had

sought a new location for games and training. They would have had no inkling that their move from People's Park would eventually see the name Stradey Park come to mean so much more than a dry entry on a local authority document.

Well before the dawn of the 2007-08 rugby season, supporters had grown to love Stradey Park, their memories of the place and the sporting heritage it represented.

It had seen league wins and legends, cup glory and craftsmanship. It had brought depths of despair for home and away supporters; it had brought flashes of brilliance and times of great joy.

More than anything, it had become a glorious social gathering place for the people of Llanelli and West Wales. They sang there, ate there, drank there, celebrated and sulked there. They shed blood and tears at Stradey Park while working, socialising, playing and performing.

But it was time to progress. Almost 13 decades after moving in, Llanelli RFC – along with its professional brother-in-arms The Scarlets – was on the move once more.

The ground edged into its final months, yet its vitality remained. The 2007-08 fixture list would usher in the last full season of the Stradey spirit, one final, complete campaign to enjoy the faces of Stradey Park in all their great variety.

Diolch o

IT was a privilege to be invited to write this foreword. Initially that pleasure had been Ray's so, as Stradey was so close to his heart, how could I refuse?

Ray's first visit to Stradey in 1956 was on his father's shoulders, when he was five. Jack was a collier who had played for Pontyberem and Cydweli and Ray adored him, then, and for the rest of his days. Jack's ambition for his only son was that he should play for Wales. Ray's only ambition was to play for Llanelli. Sadly, Jack didn't see his boy represent Wales and the Lions yet Ray said with great conviction that when in 1975 he ran on to the Parc des Princes for his first cap he felt, was aware, *knew* that his father was there somewhere, supporting and giving strength to his nervous child. I believed him.

Ray's burning passion for Stradey was well known and he was a proud chairman of the supporters club and president of the Llanelli Scarlets. During his playing days he crash-tackled, scored, defended, joked with the ref, and received treatment from Bert Peel (Dwayne's Dadcu) in front of the old stand and Tanner Bank. You all know the stories like the one when, after a tackle, the ref told him: "That was late, Gravell" and Ray replied: "Sorry, ref, but I came as soon as I could." And the one of Bert's "red, magical pills" (actually Smarties!). Ray insisted that, like another of his heroes, Carwyn James, Bert understood people; this was certainly true in Ray's case.

As captain of Llanelli, Ray continued the Carwyn factor off the pitch; it was he that ensured that Stradey reflected its Welshness.

Clwb Rygbi Llanelli Rugby Club was his doing, without offending anyone. Pride in the ancient language was to be shared with everyone and Stradey was, in his mind, at the heart of West Wales. He succeeded to a large extent in his efforts for Stradey and I know it would be a huge disappointment to him if this pride was not transferred to our new stadium, Parc y Scarlets.

I married in red. To marry my hero in any colour of the rainbow would have been a delight, but I knew - and he knew - that there was really only one colour. We married in 1991 and his wedding present to me was a 10-year Patrons Ticket at the new North Stand. It was a present that I cherished. The late Ken Jones gave me a choice of seats. What a gentleman. I'm proud to say that even after that ticket had lapsed Ray continued his generous gesture and, in later years, both Manon and Gwenan got their own seats next to me.

The last time he played on that sloping pitch was in 2000, in a testimonial match for Rupert Moon during National Eisteddfod week. It was August and, between sword bearing duties, Ray wanted to ensure that the festival involved the Scarlets.

He was instrumental in two important outreach ventures; one involved their presence on the Maes which saw children from all over Wales meet their Scarlet heroes. Under rugby's new regionalisation plan, Ray wished dearly that Stradey would care for North Wales; the "Gogs" proved a challenge that Ray relished as he believed passionately in One Wales and possessed the uncanny knack of making that possible.

galon

Mari, Manon and Gwenan Gravell at home in Mynyddygarreg.

Ray's funeral service was at Stradey Park. Eight thousand attended on that sunny day in November 2007. He would have been immensely proud that so many had turned out for him, and on behalf of Manon, Gwenan and myself I thank everyone who made it possible. Everyone.

It was a solemn, dignified occasion and deeply emotional. Friends from all over the world congregated at Stradey to pay tribute and to celebrate the life of a very special Scarlet.

Braint yw sgrifennu'r ychydig eiriau hyn o gyflwyniad. Er mor anodd yw cydnabod y ffaith ei fod wedi ein gadael, rhaid camu 'mlaen. Dyna fyddai ei ddymuniad e'. Camu mlaen yn bersonol a cheisio cefnogi'r camau sy'n rhaid i'r 'Scarlets' eu gwneud.

Wrth fynediad newydd Parc y Scarlets, fe fydd yna gerflun o Ray, ac rwy'n mawr obeithio y bydd pawb fydd yn cerdded heibio iddo yn derbyn rhyw fath o deimlad cynnes o'r gŵr o'r Mynydd. Ys gwedodd Caryl Parry Jones yn ei chan iddo:

"Dewch lawr o'r mynyddoedd
A lan o'r dyffrynnoedd
I weiddi ag un floedd i bedwar ban byd,
Yn gri o'r Gorllewin
Cyhoeddwn fel un dyn
Mai West is Best."
Diolch o galon.

Mari Gravell
September 2008

Magic and

STRADEY Park is much more than a rugby venue; it encapsulates so much that is good, so much that is Welsh. Stradey Park is, and has been, the perfect stage on which to highlight our pride, to revel in our identity and to exhibit our fierce determination to express ourselves.

Our Region is shown fondness and respect around the world – and Stradey Park symbolises the values that created such feelings. Victories on the Stradey turf have reminded the world, over the past 129 years of constant industrial and social change, that the Region remains relevant, that with all its cultural, business and community achievements, it can't be ignored.

To play there in a visiting team (particularly in an all-white kit!) was to attempt to confront and quell the unfathomable power, magic and mystique – embodied in Scarlet jerseys - which flowed there from all parts of Welsh-speaking Wales and beyond.

"West is best", Grav told them, and so many faced with Stradey Park's unique blend of panache, passion and pride – against their will – believed it! I believe that no other rugby organisation around the world can match the way in which our Region is interwoven with its communities, culture and language.

Perversely, it was a threat to the existence of Stradey Park – and indeed the Scarlets themselves – that triggered my involvement as chairman of the board over 11 years ago. This was in the early, financially brutal days of professional rugby. By that time, chief executive Stuart Gallacher and directors Peter Jones and Ron Jones had made, against

enormous odds and with great courage and acumen, the first decisive move in the club's survival, by raising share capital and refinancing assets.

There have been many battles since, including the bitter struggle to "stand alone." Losing that – and merging with Swansea - would have signalled the end of top-flight rugby at Stradey Park. It was a battle that saw many great clubs hit hard. They included Swansea, Neath, Pontypridd, Ebbw Vale and Bridgend.

Two constants throughout the battles have been Stradey Park and the board's duty to the ground's legacy, our responsibility to all who the Scarlets represent in our Region. This duty has galvanised our efforts to survive and thrive. I believe that the Stradey Park legacy, the sheer weight and responsibility of its heritage, was the deciding factor in resisting a merger and in our subsequent determination to survive.

Hence, when realisation dawned that we could not continue building the Scarlets heritage and essential role in Welsh sport, culture and society without moving to a new state-of-the-art facility, the whole board suffered. We well remember the sleepless nights, the soul searching, the almost unbearable strain due to the sense of responsibility to this beautiful and wondrous old place. Yet, against this emotional backdrop, the cold reality was that all attempts to stay here had proved to be financially unworkable.

We needed support to move, of course. That came from our fans, the local community, our staff and – crucially – Carmarthenshire County Council. Without the local authority's incredibly professional, robust and forward-thinking approach we would simply not be heading where we are now.

The commitment of the Scarlets executive directors, Stuart Gallacher, Gareth Jenkins and

mystique

Huw Evans with his family on matchday in Stradey Park's Carwyn James Lounge.

Gareth Davies to the Scarlets, and the commitment of main board directors Tim Griffiths, Philip Davies and Granville Wise, together with the rest of the board, are directed towards one goal. That goal is to take the ethos and heritage of Stradey Park, the achievements of its past players, clubmen, supporters and sponsors - and, essentially, its Welshness - to Parc y Scarlets. Past heroics will be commemorated there, our national pride will be celebrated there, dreams will become reality there.

This duty is a massive responsibility for the board, in many ways greater than any we have shouldered in our business lives. Accordingly, we are irrevocably committed to our Region's Welshness, its people and of course to the indelible and daily memory, of our hugely valued and missed dear "brawd" Grav. Like no other, he was and remains at the pinnacle of all that true Welshmen and Scarlets aspire to be.

Huw Evans
Chairman of the Scarlets board
September 2008

Thanks

THE idea for Faces of Stradey Park was simple – a snapshot of life at Stradey Park during its final full season. Yet the process turned out to be much more complex than we'd anticipated. It was nobody's fault; it's just that this rugby ground is a place of the most astonishing contrasts.

The memories of its people stretch back to the 1920s yet the Scarlets business is geared to the 2020s and beyond. The pitch first hosted a game in 1879, yet the groundsman's skill is bolstered by technology of a much more savvy age. The individuals who populate Stradey Park at various times each week - especially on matchday - represent the widest imaginable social spectrum.

So how to distil such variety into around 160 pages? Well, with a great deal of assistance from a great number of Stradey Park folk – that's how.

So, whether you welcomed us into your home or workplace for an interview or dredged your memory banks for anecdotes, we thank you.

If you spent hours with us or just posed for a 20-second photo like those pictured above, we thank you. We thank those who physically, financially and skilfully helped to create the book.

Llanelli RFC and the Scarlets are lucky to have one of rugby's most remarkable and enthusiastic sports historians amongst their support and his input - although he'd modestly disagree - was crucial and very welcome. Thank you, Les Williams.

Most of all, thanks to our families who lost us for many long periods throughout 2007 and 2008. This book is dedicated to you.

Enjoy the book ... and enjoy Parc y Scarlets!

Andy Pearson and Terry Morris
September 2008

Documenting history

Terry Morris

Andy Pearson

FACES of Stradey Park is the second book by photographer Terry Morris and writer Andy Pearson.

In 2006 they won applause for Cool Cymru Collection, a fly-on-the-wall look at how Morris created Wales' first photographic hall of fame. The adventure included photoshoots and interviews with cultural icons such as Dame Shirley Bassey, Joe Calzaghe, Ioan Gruffudd and Bryn Terfel.

Llanelli born and raised, Morris is a respected documentary photographer and one of the UK's finest portrait specialists. He has worked around the world.

In 2005 he became determined to revive the role of photography as an art. He fashioned the hall of fame, securing sittings with high-profile stars who had brought global recognition to Wales.

The Wales Millennium Centre launched the Cool Cymru Collection, making Morris the first photographer to exhibit there. A documentary series charting the collection's evolution was broadcast by ITV Wales.

Morris lives in Llanelli with his partner Laura. He has a son, Conor, and a daughter, Sadie May.

Pearson is a writer and media consultant who spent 23 years as a newspaper journalist. As well as taking the Llanelli Star to several national awards as editor from 2002 to 2006, he worked as a reporter and sub-editor for the Western Mail and as features editor on Wales' biggest selling newspaper, the South Wales Evening Post.

In the late 1990s he was a key driver in the launch and development of a series of nostalgia books that topped South Wales sales charts. Born in Brecon, Pearson lives in Swansea with wife Claire, son Evan and daughter Millie.

A pride of

A LEGEND, every one, beneath the red and white Stradey Park goalposts. Treading the world-famous turf together for one final time, these 14 men played for the British Lions whilst on Stradey's books.

Between them – from Bynea's Terry Davies to today's Scarlets captain Simon Easterby – they toured in every decade from the 1950s to the present day. Indeed, only two living Llanelli Lions are absent (due to foreign travel).

From Llanelli all reached the pinnacle of British and Irish rugby. Now they've been gathered by Scott Quinnell on behalf of the Scarlets who are eager to take an historic photograph as Stradey Park enters its final, emotional months.

The gathering takes place as the early evening sun of May 2008 burns above the North Dock. Tommy David says: "It's special to come to Stradey and to see mates I played with, drank with, represented Wales with, toured with … and kicked the hell out of in training.

"Looking at the great players here today makes me realise that life moves on quickly. It's great to bring back memories of all the

fans and all the people on the committee. To look at the people around me today, I know I've been a very lucky man."

JJ Williams says: "When you meet here, you realise how lucky you were to play with such wonderful players. In the 1974 Lions four of us were there, and when you see others like Delme Thomas, the Quinnell boys, Ieuan Evans and Terry Davies it shows what a great club this is. To be one of the Llanelli Lions is special."

So can JJ distil his memories of Stradey Park into one word?

"For me there's one word that sums up Llanelli rugby and that is 'flair'," he says.

Scarlet Lions

"We produced players with exceptional flair – wherever we went in the 1970s we played fabulous, exciting, open rugby."

And one character?

"Phil Bennett," says JJ. "When I was here, he was the orchestra and all the rugby was played around him. He played an off-the-cuff game and supporters would pay to see that. He was a local man, he was a brilliant player, he played his best rugby at Stradey and he was idolised."

Delme Thomas says: "To look back at this photograph in years to come will be wonderful. Stradey Park is where I played all my rugby – Stradey Park is everything to me."

Back together on home turf — 14 players who were British Lions whilst on the Stradey Park books. Pictured in May 2008, they are, from left: Peter Morgan (toured 1980), Gareth Jenkins (2005 as coach), Simon Easterby (2005), Delme Thomas (1966, 68, 71), Derek Quinnell (1971, 77, 80), Roy Bergiers (1974), Terry Davies (1959), Tommy David (1974), Robin McBryde (2001), Scott Quinnell (2001), JJ Williams (1974, 77), Ieuan Evans (1989, 93, 97), Phil Bennett (1974, 77 as captain) and Dwayne Peel (2005). The two other living Llanelli Lions were not present. They were Lewis Jones (1950) and D Ken Jones (1962).

Going to the match

Suzanne Davies, one of the Stradey Park
Family Red Zone's face painters.

Maes-y-Coed: it's our catwalk

Observation
Scarlets v Dragons

PAST the grey Llanelli Electricity and Welfare Club they come - between the red brick semis and faceless Trans World House; the chattering straggles of rugby lovers in Sunday brogues, chunky boots and beloved trainers. Guided by lines of angular police cones, they trek animatedly towards their second home.

Maes-y-Coed is a 200-yard strip of patched-up tarmac that leads to the main gates of Stradey Park; it's the supporters' rich red carpet, their catwalk. And today it reveals that Scarlets fans – in a rainbow of social hues – are no walking advertisement for the world's haute couture houses.

All shapes and sizes walk up this road; all ages, all classes.

It's where fitness freak mixes with the infirm and where veggies rub shoulders with burger lovers. Like figures in Lowry's painting, Going to the Match, they're brimful of expectation – partly in anticipation of the game, largely because of the great coming together that two or three hours at Stradey Park means. There'll be banter, beer and the blowing away of cobwebs. As competition commences in the 2007-08 season, the Newport Gwent Dragons bring some black-shirted followers who speckle the red. Supporters stride up Maes-y-Coed, Iscoed and Stradey Park Avenue in a medley of hope and doubt.

They sport the latest jerseys of Wales, the Scarlets and the Lions. They advertise Tetley's, WRW, Brains and Zurich. Retro items offer a less overtly commercial spectacle.

It's a warm September day so there are T-shirts from the club store and Top Shop; there are polos with fire-breathing dragons, Rolling Stones lips and slogans – "I'm as confused as a baby in a topless bar."

19

There are blue T-shirts yelling "Italia!" and yellow favourites backing Brazil. Most legs are clad in denim – embroidered, ripped, blue, indigo, baggy, boot-cut, stretch, Levi's, Wrangler, Lee Cooper, Diesel, Asda. Shirts are worn outside the jeans; some prefer the more formal look. Some even have ties, although you suspect these are club officials, or corporate guests fearing that tickets will be valid only with appropriate neckwear.

There's the occasional fleece, some flat caps, one or two hoodies and a few soccer tops from Liverpool and Manchester United. They're red, which helps.

There are hats too – peaked red items with the Scarlets badge, beige models and navy beanies. Baseball caps promote New York, Marvel Comics and the Yankees. Others carry a maker's name – Le Coq, Reebok, Nike, Diadora, Quiksilver. Some are more cryptic – USA 01, EST 1982, Safari Tours, Talent Scout. Explorer hats have made it back from summer hols. Cowboy hat count: one.

The Maes-y-Coed catwalk may be short on Valentino shades and Lacroix handbags, but this is where life is real, where the spirit is more than a fashion.

A week ago, at the Bath friendly, there were sunspecs, knee-length skirts and vest-tops. There were Hawaiian shirts, three-quarter length combats, long surf shorts and fast-tiring holiday sandals.

Young girls wore delicate cottons, boys their tie-dye T-shirts and Scarlets polo shirts.

Two young girls arrived with their sharp-dressed dad. Gwenan and Manon Gravell - like so many others - had new-issue Scarlets tops and blue jeans with summer sandals.

Dad was one of the smartest in the ground – okay, his New Balance trainers had seen a few miles, and his khaki cargos may not have been standard issue for club president – but his freshly pressed, light blue, short-sleeve cotton Oxford was immaculate, and his club tie had been knotted with diligence. There were few who matched the style of Grav on the day of his benefit game.

Today, however, it's time for the real business to begin. The Magners League is back and Stradey Park is looking as smart as its most celebrated outside centre.

The names of streets around Stradey Park became familiar to rugby fans around the world.

D CHAPMAN
RWAIN I THE WILLOWS
MAN STREET
DING TO THE WILLOWS

MAESYCOED

DENHAM AVENUE

LAN PARC Y STRA
ADEY PARK AVENUE

D CHAPMAN
MAN STREET

PEMBREY RD.

STRYD STEWART
STEWART STREET

BRETTENHAM ST.

ST.

HEOL NEWYDD
NEW ROAD

ISCOED

Aron Evans, of Llangennech, celebrates his 10th birthday with pals in the Family Red Zone marquee before September's Magners League clash with Connacht. It was a double celebration, as the Scarlets won 34-11.

The smell of success

Observation
Scarlets v Bath

THE greengrocer's been doing good business again. His onions are sizzling in the burger vans outside the South Stand; the smoke's mingling with the crowds. The tangs weave around the meaty eddies of the hog roast.

There's a tempting waft of deep-fat chips; beer fumes rise from firmly gripped plastic vessels. Sweet popcorn and bags of sticky chews add to the cacophony of smell.

There's a woodland haven between here and the admin block. Tall pines reach for the summer clouds and cocoon the ticket office in Radox perfume. The food fragrances are out-muscled by nature once more beyond the modest white marquee where players and officials will gather in a couple of hours for post-match food.

Here today, the Stradey Park training pitches are alive with shouts and laughter as dozens of young tag players do battle. They've travelled from as far away as Pembroke Dock and they're clad in bright blue, deep blue, claret and black, yellow and red. Face painters have been at work, with dragons and "Scarlets" rouged on many young faces.

The changing rooms emit a gleeful wintergreen bouquet. The visitors' coach arrives and throws out a few gulps of diesel.

Through a creaking, iron turnstile, there are more essences to heighten the Stradey experience. The pitch has its own sweet nature - it offers the ravishing scent of freshly-mown turf.

Young mums look on in their personal clouds of Chanel, Christina Aguilera and Agent Provocateur. The dads? They're all Lynx and sun cream, left over from Majorca and the Greek Islands.

Some who've bought a programme sink their noses into a centre spread bathed in the agreeable whiff of a printing process at

Llandysul's Gomer Press. The Town End Tavern's had a new lick of creosote and this competes with the terracing's earthy concrete perfume and the hint of sea breeze coming in over Sandy Road. Gone, in this new age of smoking bans, are the sweet curls of pipe smoke and the less welcoming whiffs from cigar and cigarette. A bonfire night gasp of firework fumes clears after the arrival of the players - yet the onion trails persist.

However, it's the heady aroma of the grass that leaves the deepest impression. Wherever you are in Stradey Park, the vast swathe of green can be felt by its incense. What other stage could possibly offer such a heady perfume?

The colours are ravishing too. The variety is like that of an artist's palette. From the delicious green pitch and its clean-cut white lines spins a swirling union of colour. There's much vibrant red, of course, in the shirts of players and fans and in the animated scarlet presence of mascot Cochyn. The brick-built base of the scoreboard is painted bright red as is the nearby TV studio box and the police box at the Pwll End.

The thousands of red seats are complemented by the grey of the concrete steps and terracing, the metal covers of the stands and – today – by a sea fret billowing in over the semi-detached rooftops of Denham Avenue. Bright yellow is prominent

Anticipation builds near the Scarlets Social Club before a December 2007 kick-off against the Ospreys, left, and other familiar sights around the perimeter of the ground.

– on stand and terrace steps, on handrails and safety fencing. Blue's in short supply, although there's a glorious sky and Bath have a stylish shade on their shirts.

The whites include upright pillars, proudly shouldering the roofs on three sides of the ground. Look closer and you'll see that the inside edges of the girders are a dusty grey. The top half of the goalposts are white too, with the red ground-level sections cushioned by blue pads.

There's a trimming of black, including painted letters at the back of the South Stand that are a little rough at the edges, flaking where once a steady hand crafted them with great deliberation. In the South Stand,

generations of painters have left red and yellow dribbles and splats on concrete steps. They reveal how human endeavour has shaped this structure. The metal tubes that form the skeleton of the fading South Stand seats are showing their age – black paint gently flaking at the pressure points.

The red brick wall that separates the South Stand from its enclosure is topped with solid beams that reveal how deep the red runs around here. Yes, it's peeling in places, but it's built of multiple layers.

Black numbers stamped on the South Stand seats suffer from the wear of generations of coats, jumpers, T-shirts, sweaters and replica tops – many digits are

indistinguishable or missing. The whole ground feels refreshed by new licks of ground staff paint and by a kaleidoscope of colour provided by advertising boards.

At the Pwll End there's the smart white of Stena Line, C&C Insurance Brokers, CSA and Veolia Environmental Services. The North Stand has splashes of bright white thanks to supporters such as Cawdor Cars, Specsavers and OJ Williams of St Clears. Darlows and Carmarthenshire Council have injected white at the Town End. Blues are added by the JVH Group, Tetley's, GenSet and WRW.

They might love their scarlet down Stradey – but it's not the only colour there.

As excitement mounts for family fans, an autograph from Ray Gravell tops the day for 12-year-old Iestyn James, of Rhydowen, near Llandysul.

Stradey Park's floodlights tower
over the rooftops of Llanelli.

Going to Stradey -
part of growing up for
young sports lovers.

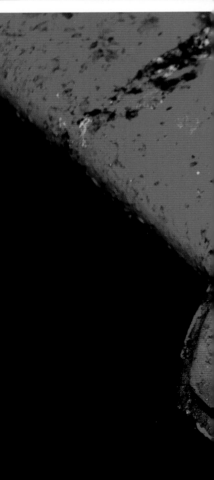

Turnstiles
that served
Stradey Park for
generations.

Food, drink, friendship

A burger van outside the South Stand's Scarlets Cafe does brisk business before Magners League action involving The Ospreys in December. The Scarlets won 17-12.

With cunning — that's how we should play

Observation
An annual dinner

WH Clement, Rhys Roberts (Ferryside), Bryan Thomas (Haverfordwest), DB Rees (Pembrey), Eden Evans. A mundane list of names, it may seem, but it's an indicator of a captivating human strand that runs through the history of Stradey Park.

It's a short roll call that produces murmurings of respect and smiles of recognition as it's read out at the Scarlets Former Players Association annual dinner.

One-time Llanelli, Wales and British Lions full-back Terry Davies is at the centre of the Tetley's Suite top table and his request for a minute's thought for these recently lost colleagues is honoured with a dignified silence. Only the hum of the bar electrics and a TV set's whispered commentary on the France-Argentina Rugby World Cup opener can be heard.

Around the tables are men with unbreakable ties to the heritage of their club. They include Peter Rees, Marlston Morgan, Derek Quinnell, Handel Greville, Hywel Jones, Laurance Delaney and Sean Gale.

Around 80 former players and friends represent decades stretching from the 1930s to the present; one or two are in wheelchairs or carry walking sticks, others are apparently in their prime.

Formalities are relaxed, befitting the unified nature of the event. A dress code of blazer or lounge suit is not strictly followed – and that seems right. The September humidity sweating the conifers outside the function room brings a quick removal of many jackets.

Large circular tables are draped in rich red cloths, bottles of American beer (Budweiser), Irish cider (Magners) and Danish lager (Carlsberg) crowd the centrepiece vases of delicate pink and white freesias. As the Pumas spring a surprise on the largely ignored TV set, the diners soak up flavours from the Argentinian wine region of San Juan – a 2005 shiraz malbec and a slightly younger chardonnay viognier from the Andean vineyards.

A soup starter, beef dinner (with extra roasties if desired), and cheese and biscuits appear to satisfy.

Miniatures of Gordon's Gin, Bell's whisky and Smirnoff vodka are happily decanted into shorts glasses and savoured.

Old stories are swapped, debates on the move to a new stadium reignited and thoughts on the club's slow start to the new season traded.

Comedian Bryn Phillips tells the tale of opening a show for Tommy Cooper in Dartmoor Prison. In front of scores of inmates, Cooper walked onto the stage with a stocking over his face. He told them: "I just wanted you to feel at home."

Guest speaker is rugby icon Clive Rowlands, a former Llanelli scrum-half. His theme of the journey from his home village of Upper Cwmtwrch to Stradey is developed into a powerful argument for the importance of strong clubs.

He delights his audience with tales of his home village's dual carriageway – possibly the shortest in the world – and of his local club welcoming with open arms a touring bowls squad from Bournemouth.

They were embraced with a promise that cash prizes on bingo night were much more generous for visitors than locals – with a result that the new-found friends bought plenty of bingo cards and swelled the club coffers. Then the bingo caller started … and used only Welsh. "Cunning," smiles Clive, "and that's how we must continue to play our rugby!"

His pain from demons such as childhood illness and a later battle with cancer had been fought, he says, by a solid grounding in the team spirit of Welsh rugby.

In one corner of the room is a large promo board featuring powerful photo blow-ups of current heroes in action. "Scarlets," it reads, looking out proudly onto so many of the club's past performers, "calon rygbi Cymraeg – the heart of Welsh rugby."

Marlston's wow factor

Interview
Marlston Morgan

WHEN it comes to playing host at Stradey Park, Marlston Morgan has it off to a fine art. It's October 2007 now and, as chairman of Llanelli RFC, he attends the games of both the semi-pro team and the professional outfit. He loves it with a passion, even giving tours on non-matchdays.

"The ground moves people," he says over tea in fine china cups at his Pembrey home. "I like taking them in through the patron's entrance and hearing them say 'Wow!' when they see the ground.

"Stradey Park's had so much history and heritage that once it's gone there'll always be a part of me missing, the part of me that's been involved with Stradey for more than 50 years.

"I like to take guests to the changing rooms, the doctor's room, the café and to the Carwyn James Lounge.

"If there's one thing that regularly elicits a big response it's the Stradey Park Museum because there's so much history there. Our guests see the caps and photographs going back to the 1890s and look at them with amazement. The former soldier Simon Weston couldn't believe there were caps in the museum – it had been the honour

Members of the Llanelli RFC committee in the Stradey Park Museum.

of the players to win them yet they'd still presented them to Stradey."

Weston explored the ground when making a TV show with club president Ray Gravell. But it's on matchdays that Marlston and RFC committee colleagues really thrive.

He says: "We still have a function on RFC days, and as far as the Scarlets are concerned, on matchdays we receive any special guests – they're entertained by the Scarlets, then we often take them to their seats and look after them. Sometimes we take them all the way round from the Tetley's Suite to the North Stand,

"Before that, about an hour before kick-off, we check the turnstiles, walk round and see that everything's being controlled properly. Special guests include people such as

directors of visiting teams, and committee members who come with semi-pro teams. They're given tickets and, if necessary, taken through the gates.

"After the game we entertain them. The Scarlets have a marquee near the ground's main entrance gate – at least one of our committee men refers to is as a tent! It has a bar – players and officials of both sides go there along with the referee, touch judges and assessors. We quickly find out about things happening at the Scarlets and the visiting clubs.

"Other guests we deal with might include sponsors and their friends. There can be up to 100 of them. After the game we see them back to the Tetley's Suite. We've had mayors and film stars; Charlotte Church might turn

up or Katherine Jenkins. We also host WRU officials. Back in 1977 I entertained Prince Charles here."

Marlston was born and brought up in Pembrey. His first visit to the ground came around 1949 when he was about 12 and a pupil at the old Burry Port Central School.

He says: "My father took me, catching the bus in Pembrey, getting off in West End. My father said: 'Look, there's Griff Bevan – go and see if you can carry his bags and get in for nothing!'

"If there's one thing that hooked me in to Stradey Park it was the rugby – I wanted to see the big names like Wynne Evans. I wanted to play a game on Stradey – that was my ambition when I was young. Eventually I played quite a few games there."

Corporate guests and their hosts in the Carwyn James Lounge, Tetley's Suite and the museum. Supporters represented here include the WRW Group, Dyfed Steels, Castell Howell, Tetley's and the Carmarthenshire Chamber of Commerce.

Down from the Alps they come

Interviews
Kiwi visitors

THEIR itinerary features imperial Vienna, the mighty Rhine and a sojourn in the French Alps. In Blighty their programme includes historical Bath, literary Stratford-upon-Avon and the beautiful Cotswolds. Tonight, however, they're at Stradey Park – 150 tourists from New Zealand under the sweeping Carmarthenshire rain.

They're being given a guided tour of the ground by members of the Llanelli RFC committee, followed by food, drink and entertainment in the Tetley's Suite. The welcome includes a special opening of the club shop and a rugby DVD being played on a floor-to-ceiling screen in a colourful corner of the Scarlets Social Club. It features footage of Llanelli's 1972 victory over the All Blacks.

Outside, as the Kiwis emerge from the players' tunnel, they cast an admiring view across the floodlit turf and gaze up at the scoreboard. It reads: "Llanelli 9, Seland Newydd 3."

And the silver fern tourists – in black T-shirts and All Blacks replica tops – love it. The welcome's been good at the nearby Stradey Park Hotel, they say, and the emotion they feel visiting a rugby ground of such significance is to be treasured.

It's October 2007 now and one of their guides is a man who helped regain All Black pride in the years after that Stradey reverse 35 years ago. Brian McKechnie played for New Zealand from 1977 to 1981, kicking a penalty goal that beat Wales in 1978. The penalty had come from a lineout involving an infamous dive by teammate Andy Haden – and it still hurts in this small corner of the Northern Hemisphere.

McKechnie, also a former Kiwi international cricketer, said: "To the average New Zealander, Llanelli is as well known a rugby club as any. Whenever the All Blacks lose a game we remember it … and we lost here. We've been

Rugby supporters from all over the world have fond memories of Stradey Park. They include tourists from New Zealand who gathered above the players' tunnel with Llanelli RFC committee men and Scarlets staff.

reminded of that tonight and we're happy about it because it's great for rugby – we all love the game."

His role here is to offer expert comment to tourists on trips with Young & Lee, a travel enterprise established by former All Black Dennis Young and business partner Rod Lee.

Christchurch-based McKechnie says: "There are more than 20 busloads of us here and it's good to come back to Wales. The Welsh supporters are just as passionate about the game as us Kiwis."

Sam McKinnon, of Christchurch, is a tour manager and is enjoying the Scarlets experience. She says: "To come to Stradey Park is great – I've always been told about it. I thought I'd never get here; it's such a long way for us to come. They've put the floodlights on for us – and the DVD – and it's incredible to stand at such a prominent place in rugby history."

Richard Duncan, an ex-pat Kiwi now living in Queensland, Australia, said: "Stradey Park means nostalgia. I remember sitting up the night that Llanelli beat us to shatter my beliefs about All Black rugby – we were invincible but we got beaten by a team like Llanelli. At least we'll never lose on this pitch again."

Des Krammer, of Nelson region on the South Island, says: "Stradey Park is fantastic, there's so much history here. The biggest things for me are meeting the wonderful Welsh rugby people and the ground's links with Carwyn James. I've watched every test match Wales and the Lions have played in New Zealand over the past 25 years and just to be able to come to a place like Stradey Park is special, very special – I've heard so much about the place."

Frinton McLachlan, of Northland, says: "We've come to Europe for the World Cup but Llanelli is a highlight of the trip – Stradey Park is great, a magic place.

Growing up watching Welsh greats like Gareth Edwards on TV was magic; it's a pity Wales aren't as good as they used to be. Coming to Stradey Park is quite emotional, really; walking out onto the pitch and seeing how close it is to the stands – I imagine in my mind's eye how it used to be when we'd watch New Zealand play at places like this."

Jim Presland, of North Auckland, says: "Llanelli's Carwyn James brought the Lions to New Zealand and he beat us with the top inch! We were all-physical, playing eight-man rugby but he came up with a different way of playing … and it changed the game. We never thought we'd have a few poncey Lions beating the crap out of us but they did – so Stradey's like Mecca for us."

At the end of the night, it's back to the Stradey Park Hotel, with sweet dreams of new adventures to come – in Nice, Paris and Nimes. They're also due to visit Barcelona – not much rugby tradition there, mind.

Salesi and the Martian Mallow

Observation
The Scarlets Cafe

QUESTION: Where do Spider-Man, Elvet Jones and a naked Mr Porky rub shoulders? Answer: The Scarlets Café, Stradey Park. Indeed, the comic book superhero, the 1938 British Lion wing and the bristle-bound character who promotes pork scratchings are among thousands of recognisable faces here through the 2007-08 season.

Spider-Man is one of several icons bursting from packets of candy sticks. A colourful painted caricature of Elvet dashes along a wall, together with many other Llanelli rugby legends.

Mr Porky, meanwhile, is on a backing card which carries a few remaining packets of finest West Midlands seasoned pork rind.

Elsewhere you'll find Pirates of the Caribbean movie oddball Jack Sparrow thrusting from a counter-top box of hand-decorated chocolate lollipops.

There's a representation of Salesi Finau with a helpful framed pen-pic: "DOB – 05.05.73, height – 180cm, weight – 105kg, position – centre, previous clubs – Canberra Raiders and Brisbane Tigers, Honours – 3 Tongan caps."

Packaging of sweet treats promises: Martian Mallow, Flic'n'Lic, Hi-5 Candy Power with whistle lollipop, Trolli Dracula, Gummi Candy and Rose Cream Pies – the original and best.

Not a lot of it will be on the finely-tuned, nutritionist-imposed diet of the modern rugby star.

The Town End Tavern, an ice cream van, the hog roast man and the Scarlets Cafe, complete with a generous helping of nostalgia.

THIS REFRESHMENT ROOM
WAS BUILT BY
LLANELLI & DISTRICT RUGBY SUPPORTERS CLUB
AND OFFICIALLY OPENED BY
THE PRESIDENT
D. IEUAN LODWICK ESQ. J.P.
ON
BOXING DAY 1979

Kenny Morris prepares to go on stage at the Scarlets Social Club to entertain bingo players.

Kenny's big night out

Observation
The Scarlets Social Club

AS the legends of Stradey Park look down from the walls, a reverential hush descends on the crowd. Smiles, laughter and chatter are replaced by looks of concentration. Spectacles are edged backwards; it's time to focus. Gaynor Hughes, in floral print chemise and sparkling dangly earrings, bends the mic to her lips. "One and four – 14," she deadpans. "On its own – number four; seven and six – 76 …"

It's a Saturday night in October at the Scarlets Social Club and bingo is in full swing. Around 100 customers are settled into their individual leatherette chairs and snuggled into their cushioned bench seats. Among the women there are many expertly arranged heads of white hair; among the men many treasured pints of Strongbow, Carlsberg, Guinness, Ansell's Mild and Tetley's Smoothflow. Younger visitors – in the minority – cradle bottles of Magners, Holsten Pils and cans of Pepsi. Some choose Smirnoff Ice, others prefer J2O or a Britvic fruit juice. The shorts are doing brisk business.

But refreshments are pushed aside as Gaynor breezes towards another winning line. Dobbers are dobbed – or pens pushed – and faces swiftly morph from frown to cheer, from ooh to aagh! The hum of a busy air-con unit hovers over the respectful silence. It's punctured only by an occasional smoker's rasp.

The name boards, photos, drawings and paintings continue to look on. One wall carries an authoritative wooden installation in rich mahogany. It's busy with golden, hand-crafted lettering and is titled "Llanelli Rugby Football Club founded 1872." It was, it reveals, presented by the "Llanelly & District Rugby Supporters' Club."

Beneath a simple heading – "Captains" – is a list that dates back 135 busy years to "1872-76 John H Rogers." As it advances

through the decades, its names trigger yearnings to be whisked back once more to enjoy the skills of yesterday's Stradey. FL Margrave looms large in the 1880s, Percy Lloyd in the 1890s and Danny Walters and Jack Auckland after the turn of the century.

Between Willie Watts and D Hiddlestone there's an uncomfortable gap: "World War One." The 1920s see Albert Jenkins and Ivor Jones make their mark as skippers, the 30s see Ivor still there – but the 40s are scarred: "World War Two." Other names peering out include Griff Bevan, Peter Evans, DO Brace, John Leleu, S Gallacher, Phil Bennett, Ray Gravell, Phil May and Phil Davies.

Another name board is titled "Llanelli Rugby Football Club Sportsman of the Year." It celebrates, among others: "1968 Marlston Morgan", "1981 Martin Gravelle", "1984 Laurance Delaney," and "1996 Ieuan Evans." Black and white framed photos show winners receiving their awards.

On another wall, this one wood-panelled, there are framed prints and photos of stars such as Derek Quinnell, Mark Perego and Ricky Evans. In one corner there's a lively look at Rupert Moon. "Full Moon – Rugby in the Red," states a laminated print of a book cover. It's illustrated by a gumshield grin from the one-time scrum-half, complete with battle-scarred white KooGa scrum cap. "Available from the club shop," a notice informs.

Nearby are two large cuttings from a 1972 copy of the Western Mail – an All Blacks special edition. "Llanelli toasts its 15 giants," observes one headline, "Carnival time as All Blacks fail." Another headline predicts: "The match that Llanelli will never forget."

Meanwhile, three-and-a-half decades on, the social club members are more concerned with having a good night of bingo. During a break in the action, Gaynor, from Burry Port, says she arrived as a punter but took on the number-calling three months ago. She adds: "These are great nights – the people are so friendly. As soon as I came here a couple of years ago I was immediately made welcome."

Dilys Maguire has travelled from the other side of town to be here. The 80-year-old former employee of Boots the Chemist, Morris Motors and the Fishers car

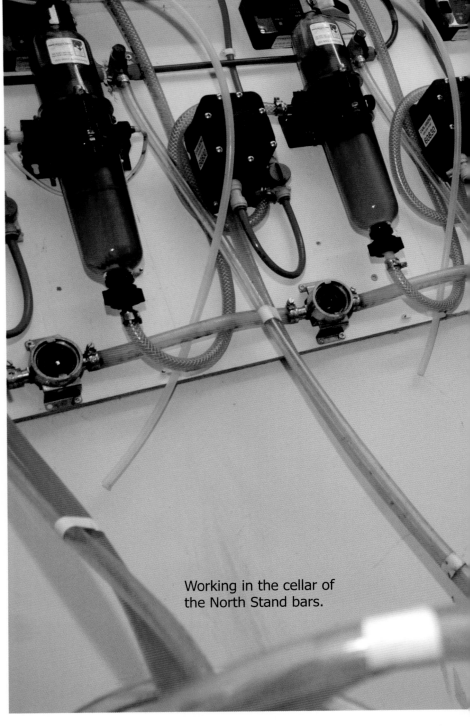

Working in the cellar of the North Stand bars.

components plant, says: "I like coming here - there's good money in the prizes. I won £120 once, although it was a good while ago. There's even a game where you can win a turkey, although you can't pick it up until Christmas."

Tonight's prizes range from £5 to £115 (plus the turkey, of course, and a bottle of whisky). There's a special draw called The Meat Raffle. Dilys adds: "There's always excitement when you win on the bingo, but I like a bit of a show too."

Which is just as well because tonight's bingo is to be followed by local boy Kenny Morris, doing a pair of music and laughter slots.

Audrey John once worked at Fishers and on the radiator production line at Morris

Motors. Now she sees old workmates at the club. The 79-year-old, from Stradey, says: "I enjoy the performers; my favourite's a black man from Cardiff – I think he's originally from Singapore. He wears gorgeous clothes, lots of fancy outfits … but I can't remember his name. When he sings he can do a bit of everything. I've been coming to the social club for 40 years, since it was in its early days. I come every Tuesday and Saturday night. It's friendly and everybody talks to you – I feel at home."

Doreen Phillips is 87 and lives in Dafen. She says: "I love the artists – the men are my favourites, I do prefer a man singing, especially ballads. Of course, the new songs will never come up to the old songs. I could

walk into this club on my own and everybody would be friendly and helpful – there's nobody in here that's stuck up … well, only one or two, but you get them everywhere."

May Shapley, 89, of Iscoed, says: "I've been coming here years – I enjoy the artists when they sing the popular songs from the TV."

Former steel erector and power worker Mike Riley recalls wonderful times at the social club, when the stage was sometimes the territory of conquering heroes rather than comics and vocalists. He says: "In the old days, before the top tier of Welsh rugby was regionalised, there were some big nights at the social club when the players came back

with the trophy after winning the Welsh Cup.

"The car park would be packed with supporters and Gareth Jenkins and the skipper would get up on the stage with the cup. The chance to take photographs of players with the cup will always be one of my huge memories – they were tremendous nights."

However, he now gets a big kick from the turns. He says: "The acts I like are those that can make you laugh without being smutty and those singers who've got a good voice so people can get up and have a dance.

"There've been so many good acts here over the years that it's difficult to choose the best – but one lad came here not so long back, he was only 16 and ended up winning

a TV talent show. He did things like Mr Bojangles – his name was Karl Morgan, I think. Some of the best talent over the years has come from the Valleys – but Kenny Morris does a good job; he's a good singer and a genuine guy. He's a local boy who's done well."

So Kenny already has something of a fan base on home soil. Having hauled his amps onto the club's low-slung corner stage and installed his stage clobber into the dressing room, he takes a break outside, chatting to a pal who needs a roll-up.

Kenny says: "I can remember coming here 30 years ago when I was just starting out in the business. On stage in those days it was just organ and drums … none of this modern technology, backing tracks and so on. A guy would play the drums after coming out of his normal day job and the organist would be a fella from the local church. I'd come along with my music and they'd read whatever tunes I'd give them to play."

So what's in store for the Llanelli faithful tonight?

"I'll play the audience," says Kenny. "This'll probably be quite an elderly group so they're not going to like bumpety-bump music; they'll probably want the more ballady type of thing, Matt Monro, Frank Sinatra."

The bingo's finished. Gaynor's electronic numbers generator has been put away safely for another few days. Her audience has time for a chat before Kenny hits the stage. Former Duport steelworker Glyn Patterson, 67, says: "We used to have fancy dress parties with prizes – they were great. Once we had seven Robin Hoods – and none of them won! The acts get changed in a little room behind the stage – it's more like a cupboard actually. It's ok if they're solo, but if they're a duo they're like sardines – we don't do trios."

Glyn's wife Patricia, 64, says: "It's the company that makes this club – and the drinking! There are a lot of special friends here; we always dress tidily to come here and we always make sure we're nicely made up."

Marlene Riley adds: "The boys used to go into the little members' lounge for a whisky – but me and a friend would stay in the main room, go to the end of the bar and have treble vodkas!"

But now the lights dim. There's a shuffle of figures moving back to their seats. With two spotlights trained on the stage, the announcement is made: "Ladies and gentlemen, please give a warm welcome to Llanelli's own Kenny Morris!"

Kenny hops onto the stage, in black dinner suit, shiny black shoes and crisp white shirt with wing collar open at the neck. The backing track glides through the intro to Save The Last Dance For Me, big in 1960 for The Drifters. But tonight it's Kenny's tune and he's off ... "You can dance ev'ry dance with the guy who gives you the eye ... "

Staff and customers in the North Stand's Scrum Bar.

67   DELME THOMAS.

68   MARLSTON MORGAN.

69   CLIVE JOHN.

0   PHILL BENNETT.

1   SELWYN WILLIAMS.

2   TONY CROCKER.

    HEFIN JENKINS.

    ANDY HILL.

    ROY THOMAS.

    ALAN JAMES

SCARLETS

PHIL MAY.
ALUN DAVIES.
LAWRENCE DELANEY
PETER MORGAN.
KERRY TOWNLEY.
ANTHONY BUCHANAN

With tender loving care

Stradey Park from the
ground's entrance in
Stradey Park Avenue.

Dai's bolt cutters and monkey wrench

Interview
Dai Jones

THERE'S a small, windowless corner of Stradey Park that appears to be part blacksmith's forge, part admin centre. It's in a long, low white structure in the corner where the Town End terrace meets the concrete access ramp for the North Enclosure. Entry is by a doorway next to a first aid snug.

Inside, an industrious aroma of paint and oil is sweetened by the whiff of turf being brought in on a gentle breeze.

Filing cabinets stand shoulder to shoulder. One's black, one's light grey and one is off-white.

One or two handles are at crooked angles; there are paint splashes and dribbles.

The cabinets have seen better days but they have been – and continue to be – useful. On one drawer there are content indicators, hand-penned thick and black: "Signs booklet/drainage" – "Accident book/ health and safety" – "Celtic Mowers" – "Turf management book."

To the left there's a sturdy workman's desk with chunky vice, Black & Decker drill and transparent plastic box marked: "40-piece tap and die set – fine carbon steel – long-handle adjustable tap wrench – T-handle tap wrench – die handle – screw driver – screw pitch gauge."

On the wall are bolt cutters, coils of plastic tubing, a monkey wrench, a metal saw, a spray-paint gun and three lawnmower blades in a neat six-point star formation.

The concrete floor is drizzled with paint; shelves carry canisters of paint, pots of screws and cans of WD-40 and John Deere multi-purpose grease.

From a thick wooden beam beneath the grey ceiling hangs a paint-specked black toilet seat. This workshop is the domain of

Dai Jones. In immaculate dark blue Scarlets KooGa windcheater, dark tracksuit bottoms and strong Karrimor trekking shoes, he's eager to share his lifelong love for the ground.

A lot of people care for the place on an emotional level – but Dai also has a hands-on role involving tender loving care.

He's the Stradey Park caretaker. He has a proud past as a Llanelli player and as a coach who's nurtured dynamic new Scarlets talent.

"I came here as a 15-year-old in the late 60s to play with Llanelli Youth," he says. "Four years later I moved up to the club's second team, Llanelli Athletic, and in the mid-70s had a few games as hooker with the firsts. I only ever wanted to play at Stradey Park."

His boyhood hero was loyal club servant, hard-as-nails hooker and Wales captain Norman Gale.

As Gale coached Llanelli with Carwyn James in the run-up to the battling 1972 victory over the All Blacks, second-teamer Dai trained with first-teamers who were about to become legends.

He recalls: "It was a hard build-up but the way Carwyn got the players ready was memorable.

"He was a gentle man but he gave each player great belief even though a lot of them were young. Another crucial thing was the pre-match team talk given by the captain, Delme Thomas.

"Ray Gravell, who played that day, was in tears because of the feeling in that talk. Afterwards, the talk of the game went on for weeks. The whole thing is something I won't forget."

Dai once played with Gravell. Other star-name teammates included Gareth Jenkins and Phil Bennett, a former colleague at the old Duport Steel works. And it's Bennett who he classes as his all-time great.

Dai says: "One great reason Stradey Park will always be special to me is the fact that it's allowed massive individual talent to shine.

"At Duport we played rugby against other industrial sides and Phil's brilliance was obvious. The other side would kick off, Phil would get the ball and our forwards wouldn't

have to cross the half-way line because he'd just jink through the opponents and score. Watching Phil in action was magic; some people say Barry John was the best, but for me, Phil was the one and only."

Dai's roles at the club have included kit manager for the semi-pro squad and coach with the schoolboys, juniors and academy players.

Big names he has helped develop include modern day heroes such as Dafydd Jones and

Gavin Evans. Now his full-time caretaker role involves dealing with many of the ground's running repairs.

He says: "The work involves lots of maintenance jobs – repairing locks, doors and lighting.

"The seats also need repairs; those in the North Stand are especially difficult because they get hit by the elements. The steel's plastic coating comes off because of the wind and the air rushing in from the sea –

Stradey Park caretaker Dai Jones at the ground's main gates in Maes-y-Coed.

there can be a good number of seats to be repaired after a match.

"There may be a human element to the problem, of course, because some people tend to lean back, put their feet on the seat-back in front and push forward. Because the structure's a bit weak, the seat-back comes off. This isn't usually a big problem after a big Scarlets match. In fact, it can be worse after a semi-pro game when there's less likelihood of somebody sitting in front of you."

This white hut isn't Dai's only base at Stradey Park. He says: "I use this as a workshop and as a store for tools like grinders and hammer drills, but I have a shared office next door and another store in the South Stand. That has spare parts such as fluorescent lighting."

The job's convenient for Dai – he lives in Sandy Road, virtually back to back with the ground.

However, he acknowledges that it's time

for the club to move on. He says: "There's great history here for Llanelli RFC and now for the professional side; the place has seen a lot of terrific matches, particularly against touring sides.

"But we've seen big soccer clubs move to new grounds and their past simply moves on with them.

"The same will happen with Llanelli rugby, but there's only one Stradey Park – and it'll always live in my memory."

Vantage points from which generations of spectators cheered on their teams and Stradey's sosban-topped goalposts.

Friday night floodlit games had an irresistible atmosphere. Here's the Scarlets' Magners League encounter with Ulster as seen from the main access passage to the centre of the South Stand. The date was October 12, the result an emphatic 32-8 victory for the home side.

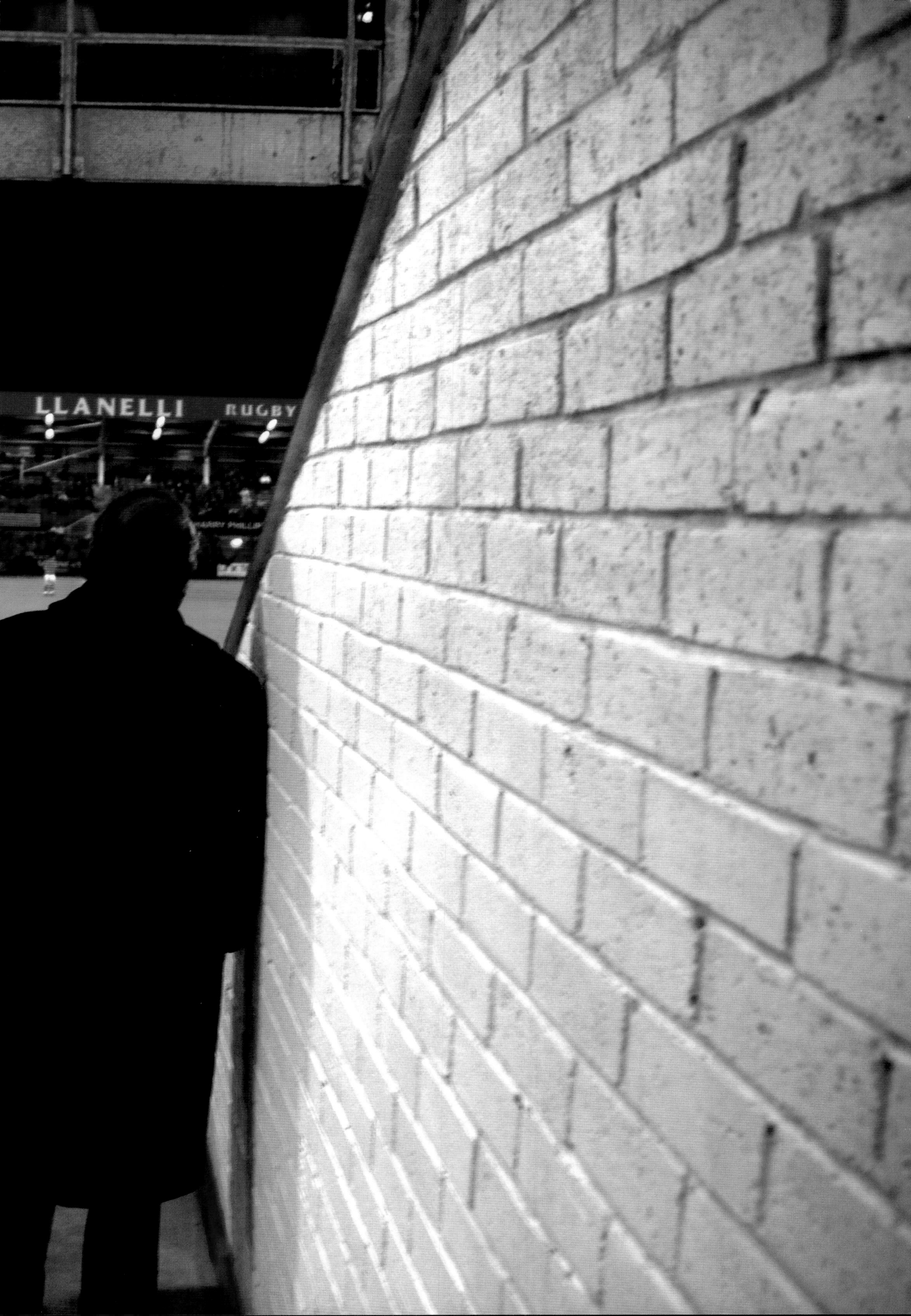
LLANELLI RUGBY

Miss Wales?
That's my wife!

Interview
Dave Healey

IT can be the little personal touches that make a house a home. The head groundsman's office at Stradey Park is small, low-ceilinged and cosy. Nostrils fill with grassy sweetness, detenderised by a bouquet of paint and grease from a neighbouring maintenance workshop.

A well-trodden grey carpet is scarred by bootprint evidence of wintry working days. Yet more lustre is masked by paint specks, nuggets of plaster, hints of earth and wisps of grass. Walls of whitewashed breezeblock and plasterboard offer typed notes, timetables and A4 sheets of phone lists; there's a year planner and a clock.

On the right is a ripple-glass three-pane window above a dusty electric heater. To the left, a wooden board holds nine small screw-hooks from which dangle keys of varied style, age and character. Their purpose is unclear to the visitor – although one hook is labelled "Fire Key."

There's a notice titled "Health and Safety Law," a couple of black plastic dustbins and, although September 2007 is progressing briskly, a ringbound calendar is stalled on July and August. It carries strangely unattractive photography of the sleek Aston Martin DB9.

There's a homespun wooden desk. It carries a paperback book – Digital Fortress by Dan Brown – a PC and recent editions of magazines such as Football and Stadium Management and Turf Business. They report: "Sports pitches everywhere have been badly affected by this record-breaking wet summer" and "St Helen's submit plans for stunning new stadium."

Beneath the desk there's a plastic basket with paperwork and a smaller wooden box with other items. Nearby, curiously, is a small Denon sound mixing desk. It was once operated on Stradey matchdays by a man who watched the rugby action on a TV

The Stradey turf ... and a machine that helped keep players on the right lines.

screen and played the appropriate tune to the crowd when there was a score. That's now done from a booth in the South Stand.

On one wall a large whiteboard is headed "POA" – plan of action. The list includes: "Do changing rooms – Post-match checks – Get bags in skip – Broken gents toilet seat, North Stand – Pitch: repair, cut."

Above a pair of wellies there's a wall cabinet with bright red doors. Inside, there's a jar of Nescafe, a sack of Tetley tea bags, a pound of sugar, mugs, plates, soup bowls, keys and padlocks. Nearby is a stainless steel sink unit and a low blue fridge branded with Lucozade Sport. There's a poster for the athletically less useful Magners cider.

A white cordless kettle waits to service five mugs. The brews can be enjoyed on one of four or five folding metal and plastic chairs. What catches the eye, though, is an image that seems at odds with this soil-and-sod setting. High on a shelf is a black and white photo in a marble-effect frame studded with

delicate beads. Smiling out from the picture is a young woman with blonde Dallas-style hair and a tiara. Across her front is a sash: "Miss Wales."

Handwritten in a bottom corner of the print is: "To my Valentine, David x."

"That's my wife," says Dave Healey. "She won the title in 1986, in Pontypridd I think it was. We were courting back then and I spent the next year being her chaperone – we had a great time!"

Tracey Rowlands had made it to the contest's final as the reigning Miss Llanelli, and scooped prizes such as cash and a holiday. Look up the Miss Wales website – www.misswales.co.uk – click on Hall of Fame and you'll see Tracey's name listed at 1986, alongside other Llanelli successes such as 2003 title winner Imogen Thomas.

After Tracey's year as Wales' resident beauty, she and Dave married. Tracey now has a masters degree in business

administration. She is a housing group's director of procurement and business management and is director of its fundraising arm.

Dave, meanwhile, is head groundsman at Stradey Park. He and a small team of hired helpers care for one of rugby's most famous few hundred square yards of turf. He loves the job and has a soft spot for his office. The hut that is Dave's workaday home remains warm, as an airy chill falls on the concrete between the Town End and the North Stand.

"This hut is our base – I can't believe how lucky I am," he grins. "I sometimes don't want to go home – it's lovely and warm and there's hot, running water. Before I came I was fully aware of the facilities so it wasn't a shock to me, but as we move forward to the new stadium we'll have new hi-tech equipment and there'll be a new office and stores for me. I'm looking forward to that." Dave is now resting his backside on the one

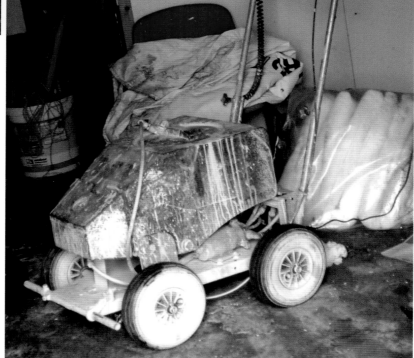

ridge that passes as a windowsill in his office. He's in a black Le Coq Sportif windcheater jacket, dark tracksuit bottoms and safety boots branded "Himalayan."

His job is to care for the Stradey Park pitch. He checks it, repairs it, nurses it, feeds it, grows it, cuts it and paints its markings.

It's a world away from your back lawn. For a start, the pitch is 100m from tryline to tryline, and 70m wide, complying with regulations. The pitch's in-goal areas are each 12m deep. Dave smiles: "Another difference between your average back garden and this is that most householders don't get two teams of 15-stone men running over their turf every week.

"Scrummaging causes me more problems than any other aspect of the game – if the weather's been bad the turf can cut up badly with the force of the boots in the scrum. That's when the skill of the groundsman is really called on, repairing that pitch and preparing it for the next fixture."

All groundsmen will tell you that every pitch needs to be nurtured to be in the best possible condition. Dave says: "This is my little green patch … and most people don't realise how much work goes into it, how many hours we spend on it. In the run-up to a Saturday match we'll be in on the Wednesday, Thursday and Friday, striping the grass with a mower or a roller to whatever width we want, adding any chemicals that need to go down and laying down markings.

"To mark the pitch takes around two hours – every line has to be marked before every Scarlets and Llanelli RFC game. We mark the pitch with a spray machine, mixing paint with water. If a game's being televised we'll double mark it for extra visibility, effectively giving the lines a second coat.

"We have stencils for the pitch's painted numbers and for the in-goal areas' Scarlets logos. I think it looks good – and 90% of my job is presentation, especially on matchday. We want the pitch to look as good as it can."

The paint, incidentally, is a special sports turf substance that's durable, doesn't harm the players and doesn't harm the grass. The grass stripes are there for a number of reasons. The design is mainly for presentation but also for guidance for the touch judges.

Straight stripes mean that officials can judge more accurately whether a player's offside or whether there's been a forward pass.

Dave adds: "When we're repairing the pitch after a game, we tend to walk down each stripe and up each stripe so we know we haven't missed anything."

The most difficult thing about preparing the turf?

"Keeping the players off it," laughs Dave. "At the end of the day, it's grass and, if anybody goes on it, it'll need repairs – divots and scars have to be replaced or put back, and the pitch needs to be levelled so there's less chance of players going over and turning their ankles.

"My biggest challenge is maintaining it day in day out to the standards required by the club and myself. Today's professional coaches understand the need for a good playing surface. They're dealing with international players and they should have the right surface.

"Once, the groundsman might have been a little cog in a big wheel; we tend to be slightly bigger cogs these days because others can see the importance of the roles that we play."

Groundsman Dave Healey prepares for another big game.

Moreover, today's pitches are far more advanced than those of the 60s or 70s; there are so many specialist chemicals, fertilisers and grass seeds that groundsmen have much more opportunity to get it right. Dave says: "There's no secret on how to look after turf; it's just making sure you have a strong maintenance programme – grass is a living plant that has to be fed in the correct manner.

"I put together a fertilising programme and use spiking and aerating routines to open up the surface in case of rain. It's also brushed and scarified regularly."

One curiosity of the Stradey Park pitch is the camber – there's a drop of around 1.5m from the highest point, at the North Enclosure-Pwll End corner, to the South Enclosure-Town End corner. With water naturally flowing downwards, wet weather tends to create problems.

Dave says: "We can get a pooling effect in some parts. To tackle that we have a verti-draining programme which we use if there could be rain the day before a game or on match day. We use a tractor-mounted device to spike the pitch at two inch intervals down to a depth of eight to ten inches.

"This opens up the surface and means that water won't hold there. The spikes are about as thick as my fingers. We do the whole pitch in seven to eight hours. We keep in touch with the weather forecasts and if it looks like there could be rain the day before a match we'll verti-drain just to open up the pitch."

So who else influences the look and condition of this treasured turf?

"I have regular discussions with the coach," says Dave. "It's a key part of my job to tackle any issues brought up at those meetings. I try to ensure they're carried out to the standard the coach requires.

There's only one person I've really got to please in this job … that's the coach."

With the quality of the playing surface over the past couple of years, nobody begrudges Dave Healey the luxury of hailing from Swansea. Indeed, many Scarlets fans have remarked on the quality he has brought to the turf and other elements of the stadium.

As well as caring for the main pitch, Dave looks after the two training pitches behind the Pwll End.

He and his team also carry out pre- and post-match checks of the ground, paying special attention to health and safety requirements.

He's tasked with the stadium's cleaning and with looking after its cosmetic appearance, including painting the walls and key parts of the terraces. For the 2007-08 season there was some special attention given to such matters.

He says: "We spruced up the ground's overall appearance, painting a sea of red and ensuring that safety features were painted yellow.

"We tried to brighten it up for the supporters and the people who work here – we take great pride in the job and where we work and, although she's an old ground, a little bit of maintenance and tender loving care goes a long way with Stradey Park. I know from what supporters have said that our efforts have been appreciated."

When he joined the Scarlets in July 2006, the club staged a European soccer game for Llanelli FC – and that meant a little drama with the iconic rugby posts. Dave says: "We had to take them down to extend the pitch. There were a few eyebrows raised because they'd never been down."

The rugby posts, seen to wave when the breeze whips up, are made of steel. Dave's team painted them when they were down, along with the iconic sosbans which measure around 18in wide by around a foot high. He says: "The posts take very little maintenance – just a little touching up of the paintwork."

A move to a new ground will mean big changes for Dave. He says: "Everything will be nice and new, clean and shiny – and you'd expect it to be like that for some years."

The materials of Llanelli legend – concrete, steel, plastic and power.

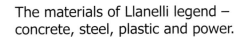

CAR PARK
£3.00

HOME

MYN...
STA
ENTR
Y WASG

⚠ Mind your head

From parking to programmes, signs spread the message.

GATE 7

MAXIMUSCLE

MATCH DAY T
& PROGRAMM
CASH ON

MATCH DAY PRICES

Season 2007 - 2008

Patrons	£32.00
Adult Stand	£24.00
Concession Stand	£18.00
Junior Stand	£18.00
Family Adult Stand	£17.00

The work of a different age

Observation
Scarlets v Connacht

HUNDREDS of bright young graphic designers work in Wales' flourishing creative industries. They use cutting edge software to produce stylish magazines, eye-catching ads, elegant logos, smart brochures … and beautiful signage.

Few of them would dare present a client with a portfolio of signs that matches the variety on view at Stradey Park. For much of this is work of a different age, work that was largely hand-painted, hand-drawn and, over the years, lovingly touched up.

Yes, there are some modern pointers on precision-cut tablets of plastic – but it's not these that will be remembered.

There are time-served signs that have been here for generations, permanent objects of a newer vintage and temporary objects that appear to have become permanent – note the large Chris Wyatt 2006-07 benefit reminder outside the South Stand.

One-off notices flourish (Scarlets v Bath – This is an all to pay match); these will appear and disappear as the season progresses.

At the ground's main entrance leans a 3ft-high wooden board bearing the cartoon face of a chirpy chef. "Scarlets Café," he announces. Breakfast, lunches, chips, tea, coffee and burgers are branded "all day" although the café's only flagged up as being "open till 2pm."

A neighbouring breezeblock wall hosts a large red panel with determined white lettering: "Scarlets Zone Family Entertainment." Above it rises a beacon of red with the club's dragon logo, the name of sponsor WRW and mention of the next home match – Ulster, October 12. Behind this, on a top corner of the South Stand's ridged exterior is a Tetley's logo in the shape of a rugby ball, and the unmissable red of "Welcome to Stradey Park – Creoso i Barc y Strade."

Further along the stadium's outer wall there are smart, computer-generated white panels announcing "Turnstile 18", "Mynediad Stand Entrance A", "Gate 4" and "Mynedfa Stand Entrance 16, Y Wasg/Press".

The two-tier changing room and bar block could be a comprehensive school prefab were it not for large sponsor messages from the likes of The Towers, Dyfed Steels and ABL. At the top there's an aged "Clwb Rygbi Llanelli Rugby Football Club."

Above a short row of car parking spaces are letterbox-size red and white name boards for the director of rugby, team manager, captain, referee, Llanelli RFC chairman, doctor and physio. Outside the East Terrace there's an expansive piece of signage surrounding a small serving hatch. "Matchday tickets and programme sales," it announces, yellow on red. "Cash only." There follows a definitive list of 2007-08 entrance fees – from Junior Field East Terrace at £2 to Patrons at £32.

Beneath a narrow corrugated steel overhang, in red on white, is a beautifully hand-scripted "N Stand Juniors £5." It's cracked across the top left corner.

Inside the ground, jostling for attention alongside the health-and-safety-happy "Exit", "Fire point" and "No smoking" efforts are traditional favourites. There are the bold black

QUANTUM
www.quantum-gb.co

Geotechnical &
Civil Engineering Specialists · irce
Tel: 01554 744880

www.veolia.co.uk
tel: 01554 756 9

OLIA
ONMENTAL
VICES

WBS
LAND, PLANNING
&
INVESTMENT CRO

painted numbers on sturdy white girders at the back of the Pwll End, and similar, homespun lettering (with helpful arrows) on upright steel posts at the back of the South Stand.

There are bright white numbers on red turnstile doors and a variety of styles pointing the way to "Ladies toilet", "First aid", "Gents – Dynion".

Substantial red and white signs above the home and away benches have a modern look, and there are helpful reminders to buy programmes and to mind your head.

The clinical edge of modern stadia is absent in Stradey Park's signage; the only consistent feature today is a refreshing lack of uniformity.

With and without you – the Pwll End.

SCARLETS

Roles of the crucial crew

Monro Walters
on PA duty at
the back of the
South Stand.

I sang the anthem — solo

Interview
Monro Walters

HE makes it sound easy – but the role of Monro Walters isn't for the faint-hearted. It's his observational skill and silky voice that work in tandem with the Stradey Park scoreboard to keep supporters up to speed on match stats.

Every time points are scored and each occasion there's a change of on-field personnel, it's Monro – from a glass-fronted booth at the back of the South Stand – who informs the thousands in the stands and on the terraces.

The tools of his trade are a clipboard and pen, a pair of trusty binoculars and his microphone. It's October 2007 and, having charted the Scarlets' comfortable Magners League win over Ulster, he sits in a fast-emptying stadium and says: "By and large, things go well – but the role does have its moments.

"I remember the Ieuan Evans testimonial game here in 1995 – it featured an International Select XV against a British Isles XV and we had all the stars of the world like Jonah Lomu. I remember Lawrence Dallaglio coming across from Twickenham after just a couple of caps with England – and the ground was full with more than 13,000.

"As it was late in the year, Ieuan told me he didn't want the boys hanging round on the field getting cold before kick-off – the band would have to do the Welsh national anthem quickly. So the time came, the teams ran out and the stadium erupted. The teams lined up … but nobody had told the band they'd be needed at that stage; they'd gone.

"There was a bit of pressure but I just picked up the mic, started singing the first few bars of Hen Wlad fy Nhadau … and thankfully everybody joined in. That was a

difficult moment but we got through it with a bit of thinking on our feet."

The most difficult aspect of the job is maintaining concentration with so much going on – there's constant noise around Monro's booth, usually shouting and bellowing.

He adds: "Getting the right scorer can sometimes be tricky; a pushover try can make it very difficult to make a positive identification. Sometimes I'll go to my right and ask the opposition coaches sitting in the stand. I remember asking that question of the Dragons this season – but not even head coach Paul Turner knew. Luckily, his back-up coaches reached a consensus and I went with them."

The professional era has managed to iron out a few old glitches. Monro says: "I formerly had to go and forage for team changes before kick-off, now I'm given a sheet with the teams – that takes some pressure off. I make sure I'm certain about the pronunciation of unfamiliar names, especially those of the Italian, French and South Pacific Islanders. I always try to get the pronunciation right if I can."

Monro took up the matchday mic for the start of the 1995-96 campaign. His father, Glyn, had done it before for many years, including the Carwyn James era.

Monro says: "My father died of cancer towards the end of the 94-95 season. The club started making inquiries about getting someone to take over on PA – I never bothered even though others said I sounded like my dad and that I should have a go. So I did. As far as I know I was the only one to apply, the only one daft enough to do so.

"My first game was supposed to be Swansea – in those days on August bank holiday – but it was cancelled because the Welsh team had a get-together. As it turned out my first game here, in the first week of September, was against Abertillery – and where are they now? It gives you an idea of how Welsh rugby has changed so much in such a short time.

"During those first few seasons I more or less had carte blanche. I sorted things out with a timetable but, walking to the ground, supporters would give me notes left, right

The Town End TV studio and other Stradey locations. The pictures show, clockwise from above, ballboys in the kit room deep beneath the South Stand, Scarlets managers in the Carwyn James Lounge and supporters with staff in the Scarlets Shop.

and centre asking me to make special announcements. We manage that a lot better now."

Things are slick and efficient these days, making Monro's life easier.

The technical side of the PA is looked after by Swansea-based sound system specialists JD-International Sound Hire. Today, the company's Jez Dabbs is at the PA booth's control panel. After Scarlets scores he plays a thumping, bass-heavy blast of the Dafydd Iwan number Yma o Hyd and a funked up version of Sosban Fach.

Meanwhile, back from his PA duties on the pitch is Tommo, also known as Andrew Thomas, a presenter on Aberystwyth-based Radio Ceredigion. He says: "About half an hour before kick-off I get taken over by the atmosphere and try to bring a bit of oomph to the crowd, get them going. Even though

we're scripted, gift of the gab's important … and working bilingually."

Although a long-time Scarlets fan and just entering his 40s, personal commitments meant that Tommo's first visit to Stradey came only last year. He says: "I've always played football – Saturdays have been largely taken up through that and work. But last year I was asked to do some PA for the Scarlets. I'm a Cardigan boy and I know that west is best so I was delighted by that request.

"The history behind Stradey Park is amazing and to come here to work before watching a match is amazing.

"When I first arrived I got the shivers; hairs on the back of my neck stood up – I couldn't believe I was standing on such hallowed turf."

78

He needs two pairs of socks

Interview
Luke Williams

STRADEY Park's iconic scoreboard can't be described as hi-tech. It dates back to 1967 and is operated by hand from a platform of wooden planks 10ft up a narrow steel ladder. For the past two or three seasons it's been the domain of schoolboy Luke Williams who pushes open a bright red door at the back of the scoreboard half an hour before each Scarlets or Llanelli RFC kick-off.

The concrete floor at ground level is dusty and at both ends has untidy piles of name plates for teams that have visited over the years. It's here that the Combined Services mingle with Sale Sharks and where London Welsh and Llanharan rub shoulders with Leeds Tykes and Northampton Saints.

Up the ladder and through a small square opening, the teenager enters his coop.

On Luke's left is the large metallic circle of the scoreboard's chunky analogue clock; in front of him the apertures for the teams' nameplates and for numbers that indicate how many goals, tries and points have been scored.

What Luke can't see is this season's advertising on the front of the scoreboard: "Brace's – proud to be Welsh."

Above the scoreboard, strung between two white poles topped with sosban motifs is another Braces Bread reminder, this time in the shape of a rugby ball. Construction firm

WRW also has an advertising presence on the scoreboard this season.

A couple of basic stackaway chairs stand on Luke's floorboards, and numbers from nought to nine are racked up around the wall, tucked behind criss-cross steel struts, shelved on wooden beams and piled neatly on the timber deck.

Light shines in through the apertures which Luke will use as his viewfinders.

This unique red-brick and metal feature rises from the top of the low-slung Town End terrace.

It brings joy to the home fans when their team's winning and conspires to make them miserable when the visitors are up.

Luke, aged 14, lives in Felinfoel and plays for his village side's under-15 team on Sundays, usually on the wing. As the

Luke Williams at work
in the Stradey
scoreboard during
September 2007's visit
of the Dragons.

Scarlets-Leinster game nears in October 2007, he says: "This is my third season in the scoreboard.

"I was told about the job by the semi-pros paramedic and kit manager Robert Evans; he lives just up the road from me – my father knows him from rugby with Felinfoel.

"By the time I arrive before kick-off somebody's already put up the team name boards. I come in here, watch the players warm up and – after the game starts – put up the scores when they happen.

"I still get excited by the big matches. I've only missed two games since I started; not a bad record.

"So much in the scoreboard is real antique stuff; new numbers are made of plastic but the old ones are metal with a wood backing – they're really heavy."

Things don't always run smoothly. Luke smiles: "Every now and then I'll take my eye off the game for a second or two and will miss a score.

"I realise I'm behind when either there's a PA announcement that the scoreboard's wrong or when people in the crowd below start shouting and pointing at the scores. I don't shout back at them – there's no point; I just hide behind the panels and don't show my face.

"It's a bit embarrassing but I just move as fast as I can then put things right."

One obstacle he faces is a glut of requests from pals at Ysgol y Strade who ask to see games from his privileged roost.

He says: "Some come up in games but they've got to leave because I'm only allowed a maximum of two people in here – it's very small so it's right that numbers should be limited."

At half-time, Luke pops out for a short stroll to get a drink at the Scarlets Café.

Mum also helps out with the refreshments. A thankful Luke says: "When it's cold outside it can be freezing inside the scoreboard.

"On those days my mother makes me a flask of tea – it's really welcome because the winters can be bitter around here.

"I'll also wear a thick coat and a couple of pairs of socks."

The Stradey scoreboard
– inside and out.

Mascot Cochyn –
familiar to every
Stradey regular.

Boots, shirts, and laptops.

Interview
Media men

IT'S the weekend of the Pontypridd match. The Llanelli RFC matchday programme carries photos of similar publications from down the years. One dates from 1957 and is priced "Threepence." The club is still known as Llanelly and an advertisement on the programme's front cover is for "Richard Thomas, Llanelly Sports Outfitters – footballs, boots, shirts, stockings."

Two programme covers from the 80s carry ads for Richards Travel Limited. Notes accompanying the images state that the first game between the two teams was staged at Stradey Park on October 25, 1884. "Llanelli, captained by FL Margrave," we're told, "won by four goals, one try to nil."

There's a salute to Bob Penberthy, a man of 876 appearances for Ponty. Meanwhile, Llanelli RFC historian Les Williams recounts some enlightening tales in his column.

On 1902-03, he reports, "a novelty at the end of the season was a game of pushball – a popular American game never played before in Wales. The ball was huge, nearly six feet high and weighing 40lbs. A strong local team was selected to play, including Ben Davies, Danny Walters and Jack Auckland."

From December 1906, he reports: "Llanelli played South Africa at Stradey and lost 16-3. Danny Walters led the side and a crowd of about 20,000 attended. The strains of Sosban Fach were soon in evidence when Tom Evans forced his way over for a try. After the game, referee JF Marsh was the subject of a demonstration and was struck by a snowball."

From October 1908, he reports: "This was the date that added a triumphant new verse – Who beat the Wallabies? – to the club's famous battle hymn, Sosban Fach. Llanelli won 8-3. For three-quarters of the game Llanelli were in opposition territory and fully deserved their win."

Such recollections highlight the role played by the media in building and sustaining

The media report from Stradey using the Press Room, left and above, the press box and a camera position.

rugby heritage. Journalists sit in the press box, high in the centre of the South Stand.

Today's RFC game has attracted a handful of people on media duties – they include Chris Barney, Richard Thomas and Alastair Cornish. Chris knows the ground better than many newspaper folk.

"I grew up in Derwent Street, just around the corner from Stradey Park in the Gareth Jenkins era of the 80s and 90s," he says after quizzing Llanelli and Ponty coaches John Davies and Paul John in an informal post-match press conference. "On matchdays we could never park outside the house – the nearest place was probably Furnace, a mile or so away. My association with the ground

started when I was six – I came down here for a Tovali Cup final which involved Aberavon. Later I had the enormous thrill of leading out my school team here in a Dragon Cup final. You expected to play down the local park so to be told we'd be playing a final at Stradey was amazing.

"I believe that my team – Pentip – and our opponents from Morfa were the first schools to play in front of the new North Stand. I was captain and leading out my pals in front of 100 or 200 people, knowing that legends like Phil Davies, Ieuan Evans, Mark Perego and Emyr Lewis had run out of the same tunnel, gave me a tremendous buzz – it was a proud moment for a 10-year-old. We started pretty

badly, however, and were 28-0 down when one of their guys stepped up to take a conversion from in front of the posts. He missed and, amazingly, we went on to win 30-28 – I even scored a try. Even today, when I see that lad who missed the kick I like to remind him of it – although I doubt that the result hampered his master plan; whereas I went on to write for my local papers, he was Matthew Jones and went on the play soccer for Wales.

"It was a tremendous day, that first appearance at Stradey – and we played there again and won … although I can't remember who we beat."

As a fan too, Chris has great memories. He says: "In the late 80s and early 90s Llanelli played outstanding rugby with the likes of Rupert Moon, Ieuan and Carwyn Davies.

"One of the biggest games I saw was the Australia match when we beat the world champions 13-9. General memories of those days include the attendances – Stradey always seemed to be packed whether the opposition was The Wallabies or the South Wales Police.

"I'll always savour the memories of such thrills as beating The Wallabies. I sat in the front row of the North Stand that day; I ate Werther's Originals and remember Ieuan going over for his try. I embraced my father

– you can't buy memories like that. It's a great atmosphere here – I remember the old Tanner Bank and recall the old guys there singing away in their flat caps."

So what about working at Stradey? Chris says: "The press facilities aren't as great as at some of the new stadiums. The view from the press box isn't tremendous – you can't see the scoreboard, for instance, which can be a drawback for a journalist – but we're higher than most supporters so we have a decent vantage point, and there's a magical sensation just being there."

Freelance sports writer Richard Thomas is at the Ponty match for the Western Mail, Wales on Sunday, the Sunday Mirror and the

Mid Glamorgan Press Agency. He says: "I was brought up in the East Midlands and started my journalistic career at Northampton. That club regularly had Welsh tours, including games against Llanelli. I grew up thinking Stradey Park was an iconic ground – and now I know it well I really believe it is.

"One big memory I have of working in the press box came about a few years ago when Llanelli scored a try – Ieuan Evans, I think it was. The crowd went up and this man right in front of me stood up, had a heart attack, collapsed and died despite medical staff trying to resuscitate him for 40 minutes. He was carted off but the crowd were almost of the opinion that there was no tragedy involved – after all, he'd died enjoying what he was doing!"

Alastair Cornish is on his first trip to Stradey Park. The secondary school teacher is also Pontypridd RFC's official photographer, a role he's fulfilled for just over a year having followed the club for more than two decades. He attends as many matches as possible to gather action shots, feeding local newspapers. He also takes promotional photos for the club and helps keep the website up to date.

During a lull in today's second half action, as thick mist hovers above the Stradey floodlights, he says: "I'll be honest – many years ago, the first name I wrote down in a rugby annual as my favourite team was Llanelli. It was the 70s and I was about 10, growing up on the south coast of England and – with Welsh in my blood – I loved rugby and especially Welsh rugby, and Llanelli were very prominent at the time.

"I've always wanted to come to the ground and today, just walking in when there was nobody about, I thought, 'Wow, what a stadium, what a phenomenal place to be!' I've been to grounds all over the country but this place still took the breath away – just look at how massive the in-goal areas are, and look at the incredible camber on the pitch. Photography-wise today, the mist means the light's been appalling, but things have improved since the floodlights came on – and I must say we've been welcomed here, everyone's been very friendly."

In the media gaze – Ray Gravell with daughters Manon and Gwenan. Right, reporters Chris Barney and Richard Thomas in the Press Room with Pontypridd coach Paul John.

Perhaps the most famous media man to have reported regularly from Stradey Park is Harry "Scarlet" Davies. Still living near Llanelli town centre at the age of 92, Harry doesn't get to many games these days but has a proud Scarlets family link stretching back more than a century.

Sitting in a comfy armchair with the Daily Telegraph at his feet (open at the sports pages, of course), he says: "My father, Ben, played fly-half for Llanelli in the 1890s. He captained the club and played for Wales in 1895 and 1896. After his playing days ended he remained close to the club on the committee side for some years.

"I got involved briefly as a scrum-half in the early-30s – I played more regularly for Felinfoel. My connection with the ground as a reporter began later that decade. My brother, Wilf, had been the Llanelli rugby correspondent with the Post, with the adopted byline 'Scarlet'.

"I'd worked with the Llanelly Star and the Llanelly Mercury as a young reporter and when Wilf went to Fleet Street I took on his

role at Stradey. I inherited his byline and soon became known simply as Harry Scarlet."

After retiring from the Post at 65, he did a substantial amount of freelance reporting for the London papers and for radio. Some of Harry's clearest memories relate to the Tanner Bank, the site of today's North Stand. He says: "For many years it seemed to be packed – and that's where all the critics were, the real experts. There was a terrific noise that came from the bank, and the critics would shout instructions to the players and officials, some of it in language that was none too polite. To my mind, that's what gave the ground its character and atmosphere.

"There was no cover, of course; the supporters were out in the open and there were some great characters. They were mostly steelworkers, tin workers and colliers who all wore cloth caps. They reflected the character of the town at that stage, a town built on steel, tin and coal. The games were real social outlets for them."

As regards the thousands of players Harry saw, one stands head and shoulders above the rest. He smiles: "The one that still makes me delighted to have followed the Scarlets is centre Albert Jenkins. Jinks was built like a tank, he could shift, his tackling was dynamic and he played for Wales. For a man of his size, he was quite a deft mover; he had everything. He was one of the cloth cap brigade and was the idol of the Tanner Bank."

Another Llanelli great left a lasting impression. Harry recalls: "The press bench was very visible, right at the back of the stand. There was no hiding – if I'd written something the crowd didn't agree with, I'd soon hear about it. The players would have their say too.

"Ray Gravell was once running into the dressing room after a match when he looked up, saw me phoning over my copy and – before disappearing down the tunnel – he shook his fist at me and shouted up: 'Harry Scarlet – give me a good write-up or I'll jump on your bloody glasses!'

Two other key figures in the local press over the past few decades have been writer Barrie Thomas and photographer Jeff Connell. Both made their names with the Llanelli Star.

Barrie's first experiences of the ground were those of standing on the Tanner Bank as a boy alongside his grandfather in the 1950s. He says: "Living not far from Llanelli railway station, I'd walk with him along High Street, Albert Street and then the railway track to the ground's Stradey Park Avenue entrance."

Jeff says: "I used to work in the steel industry and several of my friends were involved with the Scarlets. They included Laurance Delaney, David Nicholas and Gareth Jenkins who was a boiler maker, plater and fabricator. When I saw them at Stradey they'd help me out. On one occasion I was late to a cup final at the old Cardiff Arms Park. I started running across the field and saw the team group split up after having their photo taken – I shouted to Gareth and he called them all back, saying, 'Boys – Jeff needs a cup final picture as well!' Great stuff!"

Behind the scenes at Stradey Park, including – clockwise from above – ticket office staff, half-time draw sellers, the marketing department, car park attendants, PA announcer Tommo and sound technician Jez Dabbs.

The uniform crew on matchday. They are, clockwise from above, police officers, a St John volunteer, more St John personnel and safety stewards in the North Stand before kick-off.

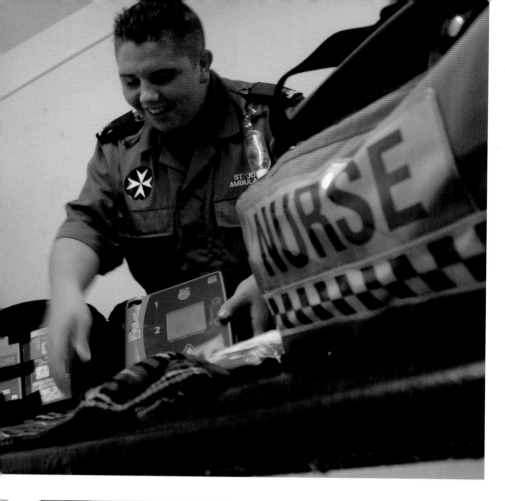

Lossin dant from Sid

Interview
Eldon Phillips

SWEET shop man Sid Richards will forever figure in the memory bank of Scarlets chaplain Eldon Phillips. It was he who gave schoolboy Eldon and his father lifts to games at Stradey Park in the 1950s. They're occasions the former vicar of Llanrhidian and Llanmadoc will never forget.

Sipping tea in a quiet corner of the Fairyhill Brasserie at Llanelli's Machynys Golf and Country Club, Eldon is animated as he recalls his early visits to the ground.

"My earliest memories of Stradey Park go back to the mid-50s when we lived in Trinity Road, down the New Dock area of Llanelli," he says. "My father was a season ticket holder in the stand. I remember very well indeed that for a short while as a very small boy of six and seven we'd be picked up by Mr Sid Richards who kept Gale's sweet shop at the end of New Dock Road and he'd pick me and my dad up in an Austin A30 or Standard 10 and off we'd go.

"His season ticket was on the seat next to my father's; the seats were planks in those days and because I was so small I could sit between them. The thrill of just being there was so great and stand tickets were like gold dust – there was only the one stand at the time.

"Mr Richards used to bring sweets from his shop and he'd share them out during the game. Sweets in those days were kept in big jars and were always sold in small white paper bags – and Mr Richards would mix them up: there'd be lossin dant, the famous Welsh mints, boiled sweets, wine gums and occasionally, to keep me happy, Black Jacks, Trebor chews and gobstoppers.

"The players I remember from those days included the great winger

The Stradey Park turf from the South Stand TV gantry at the start of the ground's final full season.

Ray Williams, Cyril Davies, Dennis Evans, Carwyn James and the great RS Williams, the Wales second row. There was Terry Davies at full-back. They were my earliest heroes. It was a great privilege to be there to watch these players."

As the 60s dawned, Eldon's relationship with Stradey Park evolved. Not only did he want to be a supporter, but he resolved to become more useful to the club, clinching a prized role as a programme seller.

"When I got old enough to go on my own I really wanted to sell programmes and I got on the team of sellers," he recalls. "However, you had to serve an 'apprenticeship.' You'd start at the more isolated parts of the ground, where the flow of supporters was at its weakest, and would progress to the more populated areas: the town entrance behind the scoreboard or the main entrance by Iscoed.

"I remember the thrill of selling that first programme – it was magical. After selling up we'd be given a tip by Mr Davies, the man from the supporters' club in charge of the programme selling; not that we were professional, far from it, but we were given a certain amount of money as a reward.

"I think that Llanelli programmes have always been quite advanced and even in those days they were rather good despite being only around eight pages for the bigger games – Swansea, Cardiff and so on. For the other games, like Waterloo, Lydney or Nuneaton, they'd just be an A4 sheet folded into four pages; a front page, the teams in the middle and some comment on the back. They were quite sought-after and everybody bought programmes – they were threepence, I remember."

As Eldon and his pals grew, this also meant that their place amongst the supporters' informal hierarchy changed.

"In my mid-teens we'd play rugby in Llanelli Grammar School on Wednesday afternoons so Saturday was always free and that meant Stradey," he says. "We'd graduated then to stand at the front of the Tanner Bank – not at the back because that's where the bigger boys and the men would be.

"As time went on we moved up the bank so that by the time we were 17 or 18 and in the sixth form we felt entitled to stand near the back in our little gang. David Prescott,

whose father Harold used to be a librarian in Llanelli, was a fanatical supporter and he'd lead us to various parts of the bank."

As working life beckoned, Eldon became a teacher, first at Stebonheath Secondary Modern School for Boys and later in Llandrindod Wells, Brecon and Carmarthen. In the late 1980s he was ordained and this led to his role as Scarlets chaplain.

He says: "For a time I lived out of the area, in Brecon, and trips to Stradey were occasional. I always stood by the scoreboard. I remember that the Saturday after I was ordained I came to Stradey and I was so proud to be a vicar that I wore my dog collar.

"I got some very strange looks because a lot of people knew who I was but didn't realise I'd been ordained. I remember it vividly, it was 1989 and I was there by the scoreboard – somebody started to swear and curse but then, very apologetically, turned round and just said: 'Sorry, vicar!'

"Being chaplain at Stradey Park is a highlight for me. It's just a case of being there – it's not about ramming religion down throats, it's being a friend, a personal supporter, a confidante. Being there, I know the players well, helping out in difficult situations and joyous situations. I've conducted players' weddings, funerals of players' relations, and I've baptised the children of players, committee men and staff.

"When Simon Easterby and Matt Cardey came here they were single young men but suffered bad injuries, were in hospital for long periods and needed support. Chaplaincy comes into its own at times like that."

For the 2007-08, Eldon is also a match summariser for local radio station Scarlet FM. Another role he continues to perform is that of on-field PA announcer for semi-pro games. He says: "For a number of years, as the 'Roving Rev,' I did the mic on the field for the senior side's games. It was innovative, I interviewed people and I was a bit of a cheerleader. An Anglican vicar being a cheerleader might have seemed a bit odd but it was a great pleasure."

As with so many Llanelli followers, visits by the All Blacks remain ingrained on his mind.

"I was at Stradey in 1989 when Llanelli played New Zealand on the wettest, windiest day I can imagine," he says. "Llanelli lost

quite closely but it'll be remembered for other reasons too – a temporary stand was put up next to the Tanner Bank … and it blew away! With today's health and safety regulations the game would've been called off but the game went ahead and it was amazing."

A few years earlier, however, things had been different.

"Perhaps my greatest memory of standing on the Tanner Bank was when I was there in 1972 on that dark apocalyptic day when Llanelli beat New Zealand," says Eldon. "It appeared that the cloud cover was just above the stand at Stradey Park – it was such a dark and gloomy day yet the atmosphere was like I'd never experienced before.

"Expectation had been quite high because Carwyn James had coached the Lions to victory in New Zealand and if anyone could plot the downfall of this very strong All Blacks side, then he could. He'd put together a Llanelli side that was extremely powerful.

"Touring sides were expected to win at Stradey but the longer this game went on the more you thought Llanelli could win because they threw their bodies on the line – I've never seen such commitment from 15 rugby players."

How I missed out on history

Interview
Huw Lloyd

THE spirit of the volunteer has rarely wavered at Stradey Park. Across 12 decades of amateur rugby, the Llanelli club was built on unpaid assistance. It's how so many jobs got done – and how some roles function today. The flame continues to flicker through much of 2008.

Today, the first-aiders of St John Cymru Wales continue to provide their own brand of reassurance. Huw Lloyd – a librarian by day – is the divisional officer in charge. He explains, while greeting visitors to Hendy Library, that his matchday colleagues are proud of the service they provide.

"We've been providing first aid cover, predominantly for spectators, for many years," he says. "We have a first aid post beneath the floodlight pylon at the north end of the East Terrace. It's provided by club management and is kitted out partly by the club and partly by ourselves.

"For a Scarlets game we take our own vehicle – it's used as back-up to a Welsh Ambulance Services vehicle. We get one first-aider there for every 1,000 expected supporters. We have six or seven at most Scarlets games and two or three at RFC games.

"We arrive around half an hour before a game, check everything's there and then set things up. If it's going to be a big crowd we'll be there earlier. We try to have people on each corner; they have radios provided by safety stewards – if they spot anything that needs stewards' attention we call them and vice-versa.

"The casualties we deal with include people feeling ill, children playing around and falling, and elderly spectators with chest pains; we've had one or two broken bones when people have fallen down a bank, but mainly we're talking about cuts, bruises and illnesses. There aren't many physical accidents these days because the stewarding's so good – they don't allow much horseplay.

"The peace of mind we give to the crowd is important. Those who volunteer for St John want to help the community and this is a great way of doing that."

St John arrived in Llanelli in 1915 and now has an adult membership of 20 to 25. There's a youth group as well. Weekly training sessions take place and members can attend weekend courses.

Afternoons at Stradey Park, however, aren't simply about treating casualties. Huw says: "I had a season ticket from the mid-70s to mid-90s.

"I eventually found that I was spending more time on the first aid post than I was as a spectator.

"The biggest memory I have as a fan was that I was working nights in the lab at Port Talbot steelworks around the time the 1972 New Zealand game was scheduled.

"After a hard night shift, I didn't go to the game – and that's a big regret. I should've made the effort to go down that afternoon.

"I was there in the early 80s when Phil Bennett played his last game; it was a shock – nobody knew until the end of that game when there were was an announcement on the Tannoy.

"We'd all suspected that his retirement was coming but, still, we were all disappointed that we wouldn't see him playing again.

"He was everybody's hero – his style of play made him special, he was so creative and he was a good leader; he held the team together."

Members of the Scarlets board and financial controller Colin Stroud meet in the Stradey Park Museum. By September 2008 the full board was Huw Evans, Philip Davies, Tim Griffiths, Stuart Gallacher, Gareth Davies, Ron Jones, Mike Bishop, Hefin Jenkins, Marlston Morgan, Emyr Wyn Evans, Derek Quinnell and Granville Wise.

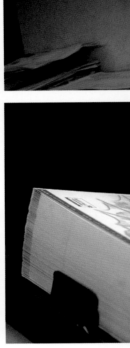

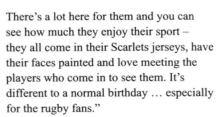

'No, you can't have my shirt'

Interviews
Unsung heroes

DOZENS of unsung heroes keep Stradey Park functioning smoothly on matchday. They include bar staff, face painters and ticket office staff.

Alison Davies is supervisor in the North Stand Patrons Bar and Scrum Bar. During the second half of 2007's Scarlets-Ulster game, she says: "I love rugby and working at Stradey Park – you never know who you're going to meet and we have a great crack with the boys, especially when they've had a few.

"Those who go in the Patrons are like a family – they all seem to know each other and they've been going there for years. A small number in the Scrum Bar can be a bit boisterous if we ever have a problem like the electrics going down – but mostly they're really good.

"I started working here about 10 years ago when a friend's father was bar manager and he was looking for staff … and it's great that I'm still there. We don't sell much in the way of food – it's only rolls and pasties – but the beer sells really well, especially the lager.

"On a matchday we'll have up to 12 people working my two bars – the maximum we had was 15 for a Heineken Cup match a few years ago. The only real problem I have is when supporters ask me to swap my blue embroidered Scarlets shirt as a souvenir – I tell them 'No – I've nothing on underneath!' They take it in good heart."

Alison also works evenings in the Tetley's Suite – for parties and other special functions. She says: "We've had birthdays for everyone from 80-year-olds to young children. At Christmas this season we've got parties for groups such as gymnasts and Mencap – there's a really wide range."

Adrienne Glendon knows all about catering for some of the Scarlets' younger fans – she's a matchday party host in the Family Red Zone marquee. She says: "I only started doing it this season and it's good seeing the children enjoying themselves.

Ticket office staff gear up for another sales rush.

There's a lot here for them and you can see how much they enjoy their sport – they all come in their Scarlets jerseys, have their faces painted and love meeting the players who come in to see them. It's different to a normal birthday … especially for the rugby fans."

The face painting is the preserve of fans such as Suzanne Davies; she decorates dozens of supporters before every home game. She says: "I've been doing it for about three years and I love it because of the atmosphere and the people. They have the Scarlets name or a dragon logo on their cheeks or foreheads, although the funniest can be the dads after they've had a couple of pints … they like having their bald heads painted."

Meanwhile, ticket office staff such as Tracey Colman can still be busy in the run-up to kick-off. She says: "The atmosphere here makes it special – it's like being home. I lived round the corner when I was younger so I've always been aware of the place. I've been a supporter but it's different again when you actually work here. It's really good when the ticket office is busy and you can see a game's selling out – that's great. The enthusiasm of the supporters wanting the tickets, and their excitement, carries you along – everyone seems to be on a high at times like that. We've got a good team in the office – we're all on the same wavelength and we enjoy each other's company."

Tracey and her ticket office colleagues have plenty of non-matchday functions to perform, including acting as a switchboard,

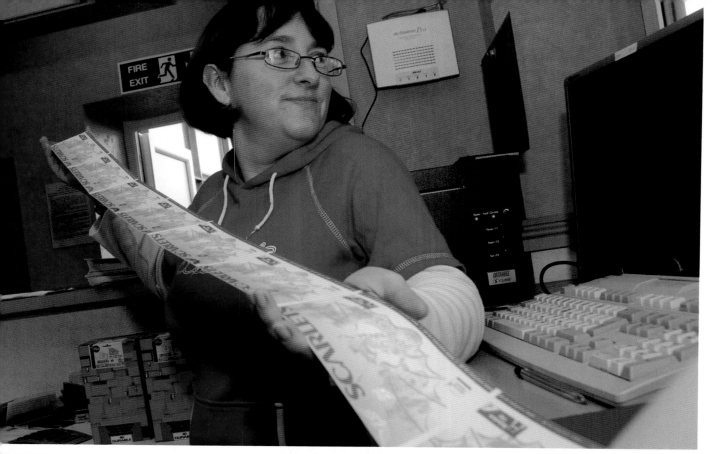

mailing out tickets and dispatching magazines, season ticket books and programmes.

Matchday programme sales are being overseen this season by Burry Port's Tony Harries. He also has duties associated with the turnstile operation and locking up.

He says: "I open all the turnstiles and close them later on, making sure the lights are off and making sure everything's shipshape before we go. I manage all the turnstile operators and programme sellers on matchday. The biggest challenge is counting the money of the programme sellers when they come back in – sometimes they're up, sometimes they're down.

"It's rare I see a game now because we're so busy counting the money. There's no real

difficulty selling programmes – everyone's looking for them.

"We can sell anything from 4,000 to 9,000 before a game – and it's all very entertaining."

His turnstile operators include Bethan Jones who's been ushering fans through for around two years.

She says: "I come down for all the RFC and Scarlets game – we meet people, get to see the game and get a little money.

"The most difficult thing is people complaining when I tell them they're not allowed through my turnstile because it's the wrong one for their ticket – all I can do is be polite.

"I've had some people trying to cheat their way in. I've seen some fake tickets that were pathetic efforts, so easy to spot – they just

looked like pieces of card."

Gate receipts are bolstered by matchday sales of items such as 50-50 half-time draw tickets.

50-50 manager Carol Cooper says: "We sell the Scarlets Touchdown Lottery tickets five days a week – we go round the houses locally, up to Carmarthen and Ammanford, and do places such as pubs and newsagents as far afield as St David's and Aberystwyth."

50-50 seller Jayne Williams adds: "It's money towards the youngsters – half of what we sell goes to help run the Academy.

"On a personal level, the buzz I get from selling the tickets is keeping in contact with all my old friends who come down and support the Scarlets."

Big Brother at the Pwll End

Interviews
Safety stewards

IT'S one of TV's success stories – but it's a little known fact that Big Brother owes much to Stradey Park. Such is the excitement of the placard-waving small screen fans outside the show's goldfish-bowl house that security is always needed.

And that's where Damian Davies and his colleagues at Safestyle Security Services come in. Carrying out duties for Channel 4, they use the valuable lessons they've learned at events such as Scarlets games.

Burry Port-based Damian is among those safety stewards who've been close to the action in West Wales and at the other end of the M4. He says: "They only let a few hundred people near the Big Brother house, in the cheering crowds behind barriers that you see on TV. Me and a few others will look after a pen of 50 people, doing searches before the fans go in.

"We also look after the presenters Dermot O'Leary and Davina McCall. We met a lot of the other celebrities involved too. John McCririck's the best – I said hello to him and we had a little chat, as you do. I asked him if he'd want to go back into the house after his experience in the celebrity version of the show – and as he was talking to me he was still doing his tic-tacs; he couldn't help himself, his arms and hands were everywhere.

"I met Russell Brand – he's just an header, full stop – a nice guy who comes over a bit big headed on TV but he's ok. I talked to him about his hair – asked him who his hairdresser was, but he said it was top secret!"

Safestyle work venues such as Wembley Stadium, Ninian Park, the Liberty Stadium and Ascot.

Damian's first game at Stradey Park was a Llanelli-Swansea fixture shortly before regionalisation. He says: "It wasn't a bad game, a bit rough as you'd expect. I think Paul Moriarty and Robert Jones were playing.

"This is a good stadium to work, especially for somebody local like myself. After working so many years here I seem to know everyone. I like the barmy army boys in the North Enclosure, especially when they sing. The vocals are good and they give the opposition, referee and touch judges plenty of friendly advice.

"The biggest challenge in this job is when you get a call that a fire alarm's gone off – it's really just a case of being on your guard and being vigilant."

Today, for the Magners League visit of Ulster, Damian's on crutches and is detailed to the security box at the back of the Pwll End. He explains: "I did my ligaments and cartilage playing for Burry Port RFC. I should've given up two years ago after an operation, but it now looks like I'll be on my fifth operation next week.

"The boss has let me sit down in the warmth today. The box is plain and simple,

you get a good view of the stadium, you see everything that's going on and can keep checks on all areas, even the Town End that's more than 100 yards away. We have supervisors in each stand so we keep in touch with them and we can control the crowd by doing our job well.

"You rarely get trouble at Stradey Park – in six or seven years of being here I've only had two incidents and they were fairly minor. One set of lads were on a stag weekend and were absolutely blathered; we asked them to leave and they went pretty quietly."

Safety steward Karen Edwards says of Stradey Park: "The people here are friendly; we rarely get hassle. I do Cardiff City as well – we do get a bit more hassle at the football."

Colleague Danny Vears adds: "I've only been in crowd control about three months – I enjoy watching the games and I love the noise of the crowd and the proximity of the players."

Safety stewards are key to the wellbeing of sports crowds. This team, from Safestyle Security Services, was on duty for the Scarlets-Ulster Magners League game in October.

SCARLETS

They all have scarlet fever

Warm jackets, a plastic pint pot and a party shop wig – the perfect combination for standing in the South Enclosure to enjoy a wintry win over the Ospreys.

OK, so I was wrong about the brown shirt

Interview
Scarlets Shop staff

CHRISTMAS starts in August at Stradey Park. That's when mums, dads, aunties, uncles and grandparents begin visiting the club shop on their long build-up to December 25.

"Yes, it comes really early," says Rhian Augustus, a sales assistant at The Scarlets Shop. "Even right at the beginning of the season people are coming in buying little things here and there to put away for December.

"The peak hits us around the end of November – it's madness! Internet orders go up three-fold and it's up to us to do all the mailing. People with family abroad order here and we ship all over the world.

"People come in and do all their Christmas shopping at once – and, as the big day draws near, they tend to come at the same time. Perhaps they've been chatting to each other, asking each other when they're going down the shop."

The shop is a modern bolt-on to the back of the South Stand, to the left of the Scarlets Social Club and in front of the stand-out red Family Zone marquee. Rhian, who lives in Furnace, is in her second spell here. She says: "There's always something to make you smile. I've been here since the end of July – I was first here in 2005 but went to live in New York, working with autistic children."

In the corner of the shop is a small fitting room, with saloon room doors and a wavy mirror. It's not as sophisticated as your average Jermyn Street gentleman's outfitter.

Rhian says, with a smile: "Customers are happy to go in there – although most of the time people choose to try things on outside the changing room. They're not going in there to try on underwear, after all – just coats, shirts and tops really. A lot of them do think the changing room's a little funny because it's so small and tucked away in the corner. When our taller customers go in there we can see their head above the doors."

Next to the changing room is the shop's storeroom. It also finds use as an office, a place to process internet orders and a workshop to put names and numbers onto rugby shirts.

"The storeroom's a real Aladdin's cave," says Rhian. "It's where all our stock is stored. It could probably do with being a little bigger, as could the rest of the shop – we have people queuing to come in on match days."

It's September 2007 now and the shop is run by dyed-in-the-wool Scarlets fan Gail Williams. She's delighted to be close to her heroes.

"I love the Scarlets and would've given my right arm to work here so I feel very lucky to have this job," she admits. "I enjoy it enormously, and sometimes do things that aren't in the job description.

"We meet so many people from around the world who are enthusiastic about coming to Stradey Park because it's got such a renowned name.

"I like to take them around to see the ground and to see the museum because I'm so proud of it all. Whenever I open a door in the centre stand to reveal the pitch in all its glory it never fails to give me a jolt, a lovely feeling. When New Zealanders come I like to see a 9-3 scoreline up on the scoreboard as a bit of fun. We've only beaten them once and it was such a big honour to do it that it's nice to be reminded every now and again."

Gail has been manager for three years and remains a passionate supporter. She says: "In the beginning it wasn't only a game, it was life or death. In recent years we've been to Northampton and Leicester and lost in the last minute and, oh God, it's terrible, terrible, terrible. It's so stupid to be so emotional but I do remember crying at Gloucester."

That was in January 2001 when the Cherry and Whites edged into a last-gasp 28-27 winning lead in a Heineken Cup game.

Back in the shop, there's a pile of mail-outs to work on. Gail says: "We've got everything from a £1 pen upwards. The coats are good

Members of the Scarlets Band make some noise.

sellers because they never wear out. The jerseys never wear out either – perhaps that's not a very good sales ploy!

"But the quality of sports merchandise now is so much better than it was a few years ago. We've got watches and we sell lots of mugs, especially to tourists. We fly through ties, especially with visitors who want to go away with a Llanelli RFC or Scarlets tie.

Cuddly toys go well, as do towels, printed bedding, children's clothes and things for babies.

"We get silver jewellery from a lady in the Bryn; she does sosban cufflinks and charm bracelets – they're marvellous, really different. There are also some slate plaques with the Scarlets badge for house numbers, they're done locally too. I try to buy local when cost allows."

Gail does the buying for the shop but

admits that it can be an inexact science. She admits: "Mistakes are made every now and again. My worst decision was to buy in some beige baseball caps with a small Scarlets logo – we just couldn't sell them.

"I was also wrong about a limited edition shirt we had in last year – they were brown and red quarters. I didn't like it but it ended up being our best seller.

"We only had around 2,000 but we could've sold thousands more. They're good for the people who've got them because they're the only shirts with both a Scarlets badge and the Llanelli RFC badge. I've only got a few children's sizes left.

"We introduced some pink clothing not so long back and I didn't think it'd sell but women and girls liked it so it sold. I still don't know what was wrong with the beige hats; I thought they were different and fresh – but there we are."

Play it again, Paul!

Interviews
The noise makers

THE man with the euphonium is brutally honest. He admits: "The band's not everybody's cup of tea, but we like to think we're contributing something to the atmosphere.

"The comments we get from fans are usually very positive but some say we're too noisy!"

Paul Evans says the band plays largely for fun, but hope they also have a useful side. He says: "We play along with the games and get a bit of singing going."

A late addition to the terrace scene at Stradey Park was the Scarlets Band.

Their drumbeat brassiness added a new dimension to matchday, complementing the PA system's announcements and recorded sounds, the fans' shouts and the songs of the North Enclosure.

Paul says: "We're predominantly members of Burry Port Town Band and we're season ticket holders at Stradey. The Scarlets Band was a natural progression of those two interests; instead of just coming along, why not make a bit of noise and get a bit of atmosphere going?

"We're as flexible as a brass band can be – we play all sorts of music – some people are better than others at playing off the cuff. Our repertoire at Stradey is traditional Welsh stuff, Yma o Hyd, Tom Jones, Sosban Fach, Calon Lan – we haven't got a fan club as such but we get a few comments online.

"Our players include drummer, Emyr Rees, who's louder than he's tall – he's only 5ft 1in

but he plays like a bloody giant. My wife's a bit manic too – Sara – she plays cornet and trumpet.

"There's also tenor horn and baritone; we normally have a couple of others but others are tied up with concerts tonight. Emyr's drum's been autographed by members of the Scarlets squad. I've been told they did it without arguing."

Brought up in Carmarthen and still living there, Paul takes a breather during the Scarlets-Leeds game and says: "We've been going since last season. I got hooked on Stradey Park around 30 years ago. The first matches I remember were those on Boxing Days in the 70s involving teams like the London Welsh. They were fantastic and featured boys like JPR, Phil Bennett and JJ."

Another colourful character at Stradey is Carolyn Hatcher, a fan since she moved to Llanelli 20 years ago. Also known as the

founder and president of Llwynhendy Women's Institute, Carol sports a decorated red and white hat that makes her a regular target of the TV cameras.

She says: "I bought it about 15 years ago, it's a jester-style thing that I've embellished with lots of badges. It now weighs more than 3lb and there are some lovely old badges there. I started buying badges from the club shop and I also brought them back from holiday. Friends have given me others.

"There are 216 badges at the moment and they make a lot of money for charity because if we have a big do I ask how many badges there are for 20p a go and I give the closest guesser a little prize."

Her favourite item is nothing to do with rugby. She says: "It's an old circular badge with the words Ministry of Health Hospital Service. It means a lot. My Auntie Rye lived with a lady called Auntie Hilda – they lived together all their lives – and this was Hilda's badge which she gave to me.

"I've no idea how old it is. Hilda had it because she'd worked in hospitals, sewing. Her mother, amazingly, had been a sewing maid to Queen Victoria's lady in waiting."

To make the hat stand up these days Carolyn has tried wire, bubble wrap and now tissue and a Scarlets fleece hat stuffed in at the top.

She says: "I'd like a new hat that could accommodate all the badges but I can't find a milliner to help. In the meantime, this hat will continue into the new stadium as long as I can take the weight. You couldn't buy it off me for all the tea in China – there's so much history and so many memories.

"Last year, me and Ernie went on a cruise to New York on the Queen Mary. There was an Ascot night and I wore this – you should've seen all the cameras flashing."

Born in Tredegar in the 1930s, Carolyn moved around the UK before settling in Llwynhendy. She says: "It's the best move we made.

"We lived in Scotland for a while and when Wales played up there I'd go into town that day just to see somebody else with a red and white scarf.

"Ernie started the mini-rugby at Ayr RFC and I remember Phil Bennett coming up

when they built a new stand there. When we arrived in Llanelli, we went to a game and stood on the Tanner Bank. The following year we got season tickets for the South Stand and we've been there ever since. We're in the front row.

"The people are special. We've made so many good friends there; Ernie's been ill this year and a great friend from Bryn – David – has taken me down.

"I enjoy the banter as much as anything; they say women are bitchy but you wanna hear the men! They talk so much about what the players are or aren't doing and they'll happily have a go at the referee."

She's seen hundreds of games at Stradey Park – but it's the memory of a match a couple of months ago that she particularly cherishes.

She says: "It was against Leeds this season and we won easily – but it stands out because of the occasion's poignancy; it was the match after Ray Gravell died.

"My last conversation with Grav was in the Tetley's Suite a few weeks before that game and he asked me 'How are you, my lovely girl?' I told him I was fed up because Ernie wouldn't let me do my shout any more.

He cringes at it because he says the voice is going. Grav just said 'You do your shout!'

"When I went in the clubhouse before the Leeds match I told them I was going to do my shout for Grav. It was a very long and very loud 'Come on!'"

From Carolyn's seat in the South Stand she can still enjoy the view she's had for years. Hills rise to the left and ahead, behind the Pwll End and North Stand, power cables span the Town End to her right.

If she were to take a seat in the North Stand for a change, she'd see the town hall dome to her left, a town centre 1960s municpal office block and the imposing rise of Bigyn Hill.

To her right would be a variety of expanded and "improved" semi-detached houses.

One has a new uPVC conservatory, there are some flat-roofed extensions, a few pitched-roof add-ons and some prefab garages. The houses are coloured white, grey and cream. Through a gap between the South Stand and Pwll End are flat faced council-built homes in grey and cream.

Wherever Carolyn sits there are the seagulls circling. Will they move to the new ground too?

Stradey styles
and smiles.

Reserved for travelling fans

Interview
Meurig Griffiths

STRADEY Park isn't remembered just for the 80-minute dramas played out on its own turf. It's also the place that many supporters have used as a launch pad for trips to other fabulous grounds across rugby-playing Europe.

Coaches line up at Stradey's expansive car parks to take them away from home for a day or three. Meurig Griffiths should know. The current treasurer of Llanelli RFC spent around a decade from the mid-90s as the supporters' transport coordinator – for both the professional and semi-pro units. It wasn't an easy job – but it's one that had its unplanned perks.

Over a cuppa and cake in his home village of Pembrey in October 2007, Meurig smiles: "I well remember a European Cup match up in Glasgow. I was on the first coach full of supporters and when we got to the gates to Hughenden a security guard asked:

'Team bus?' and I said: 'Yes' and he said: 'Follow me.' We parked up, the team bus followed … but there was no room for them! We managed to sort it out so they could get in.

"The following year the same thing happened out in France, in Agen. We arrived the day before the game, driven by a boy from Trimsaran – he'd been on many trips with us and we'd decided to have a trial run to see how long it'd take to get from the hotel to the ground.

"A security guard noticed how thorough we were being and thought we must've been the team bus. He told us where we should park when we arrived before kick-off – so that's what we did. We ended up in the space reserved for the team. When the team bus did arrive it couldn't get it in so it had to reverse out about 200 yards. Luckily, Anthony Buchanan – the team manager – laughed with us afterwards.

"Another time out in France I'd arranged to phone Stuart Gallacher, the chief exec, so he could give me tickets for around 80 of us. I called him – but discovered he was back in Llanelli ill in bed. He said Anthony had the tickets so that was fine, I thought. However, Anthony was inside the ground … you try explaining to a security guard in France

exactly who you are and who's got your tickets and why he's in the ground and why you're not!

"I tried showing him my photo ID from Stradey Park but nothing would work. I turned to Rupert Moon's mother, Audrey, who found somebody who could speak a bit of French. We could then explain that we needed to get inside the ground to get all these tickets.

"On another occasion, we were coming back from Perpignan and we had three coaches but I couldn't be on all three so I got others to check they had the right people aboard. Eventually, back in the UK, we counted 48 on one coach – we should only have had 47. Someone had been given a lift home! For all we knew we could've got through the Channel Tunnel and been counted by the officials – I don't know what would have happened then."

Meurig's links with Stradey Park stretch back decades. He says: "My first visit was 51 years ago when I was nine. It was Llanelli against Bath and it was emotional for me because I'd had hip trouble and hadn't been able to walk a lot. So going to Stradey was a big thing … and when I got there, seeing the ground and getting in there I couldn't believe

it – I'd never seen anything like it. To be honest, I'd not been out of Pembrey much, and that trip to Stradey did it for me. Ever since then it's been a big part of my life. Since then, I've had Scarlets in my blood.

"Now, I'm down there week in, week out for meetings and for up to two games on a weekend – the RFC and the Scarlets – and I still can't get enough of the place. You turn up at Stradey and it's the whole atmosphere that takes you in – the posts, the scoreboard, the whole complex. The housing tightly packed around the ground gives it a special, enclosed feel – but we've got to move on to keep pace with professional sport today.

"I'm an emotional person at the best of times, and I think I'll shed tears in the last game. When the final whistle blows I'll most likely sit down quietly for five minutes and think: 'That's it'."

In the future, of course, Meurig's memories will include many linked to those big away-days. He says: "I was asked to take over the transport co-ordinator role when European competition started in the mid-90s. Previously, we'd travelled across Wales but now we were in for a real learning experience.

"The first win we had in France saw us take a party of around 50 to Bourgoin in January 2000. To my mind, that victory ranked up there with the wins against New Zealand in 1972 and Australia in 1992 – we were the first Welsh side to win in European competition in France.

"My role involved booking the transport and hotels. I was an amateur trying to be professional but I have some great memories of how we coped.

"I remember going to see the Scarlets in Scotland – everyone was so excited because people hadn't been so far to follow Llanelli before. In the big European games we've had dozens of coaches going up, with everyone so excited and thousands of them gathering to leave from Stradey.

"Before our European semi-finals in England, we had tens of thousands going up and coaches everywhere at Stradey – as the RFC committee we had to organise these people and get them all on to the right buses. Not easy – but great fun."

The Scarlets Shop, featuring Ray Gravell and friends.

You dibbed out, ref

Observations
The real experts

THERE'S nothing like it, is there? The supporters' in-depth knowledge of the professional game's technical points … and how this understanding becomes finely-crafted informal commentary. Well, judge for yourself. A few minutes in the two Stradey Park stands produced the following passages of comment. There were plenty of grunts, groans and pauses as well – but we've left those out.

Scarlets v Ulster, South Stand

"Get in hard!"

"Good kick!"

"Go on, Matthew!"

"Hit him!"

"Oh, ref! He's lying over!"

"Out! Out! Out!"

"Ooh!"

"He's offside!"

"Referee!"

"Well done! That's the way."

"Out here – there's loads here!"

"We've got a job on with this ref, hell of a job on – we want to play rugby and he's happy to let them spoil it."

"We'll have him – we'll have him!"

"Scarrr-lets! Scarrr-lets! Scarrr-lets! Scarrr-lets!"

"Shut up! Shut up!"

"How many out today with the World Cup lot? Two half-backs, half the pack."

"Oh – it's 15 men against 16, mun!"

PA: "Gôl gosb gan Paddy Wallace – Penalty goal by Paddy Wallace."

"Run!"

"That's good!"

"Knock on! Knock on!"

"That's a penalty – we should have a penalty alright."

"Oh, he's at it again, mun!"

"No chance!"

"Go, go! Out, out! Ooh! High, mun! That's a penalty! Get him in the book, get him off, mun!"

PA: "The winning ticket in Llanelli Rugby Club Social Club raffle is ticket number 41 to 45 – 41 to 45."

"Have you won? Have a look. No?"
"No … never."

"Go on, Gavin, boy!"
"C'mon ref – he's offside!"

"No guts, no guts, no bottle – you dibbed out, ref. Oh, the number of times!"

"About time, ref! How many times?"

"Over it goes, Rhys boy."

PA burst of Dafydd Iwan's Yma o Hyd followed by: "Gôl gosb gan Rhys Priestland – Penalty goal by Rhys Priestland – Scarlets 3, Ulster 3."

Llanelli v Pontypridd, North Stand

"Go on!"

"Come on then … come here boy!"

"Get 'em, Scarlets!"

"Oh! Told you! Told you! No way, ref!"

"Go on!"

"Get him down … lost him … ooh! How'd that happen, boy?"

PA: "Sgoriwyd cais gan Nathan Strong – Try scored by Nathan Strong."

"Oh, dear."

"Go on, Jon, boy … come on! Hurray! Class!"

"Held! Held!"

"Come on, Llanelli!"

"Get to the ball, smash 'em, get in and drive 'em."

At work and at play ... Scarlets fans
at Ina Bearings, Bynea, and in the
North Stand and Enclosure.

"Oh, look at that!"

"Ooh – drive and roll ... in at the back ... go, go ... down the side ... go, go, go ... YES ... get in there ... ooh, that's better!"

"We can have 'em on this side, and the other."

"YESSS!"

PA: "Sgoriwyd cais gan Jon Davies – Try scored by Jon Davies, conversion by Daniel Evans."

"Unbelievable – we haven't been anywhere for half an hour."

"Look at that, look at this, look at this ... come on ... ooh ... ooh, dear, dear, dear!"

"Come on!"

"Oh, well done – go on, go on, go on, go, go ... ooohh!"

"Unlucky, boys."

"Tell you what, we've got 'em now ... hurray!"

"Go on, Ian boy, let 'em have it!"

"Have 'em, Ian!"

"We've got it, go on!"

"We're playing well now – go on – ooh!"

"Oh, he went over!"

"That's it, Jonny boy – show them the way, mun."

"Now switch it, now switch it!"

"Spin it out!"

"Oh ... crap, – oh, he's hurt, time out."

"Oh, here we are – here's the coach – here's The Chief again – no coaching on the field, mun."

"Here come the flying squad – how many people do they need for a little knock?"

"Look at that, look at that."

"Ooh, come on ref, for God's sake, man."

"In touch! In touch!"

"Thank you, ref."

"How many, ref?"

"And again, and again ... ooh ... no, again, again!"

"Where's he coming from, ref?"

"Come on, mun!"

"Oh, Nans, I love you ... come back; all is forgiven – you're better than this clown, mun!"

The final whistle

Observation
Scarlets v Ulster

SPRINT, they do – sprint onto the pitch, not wander, stroll or jog. Hundreds of young supporters race over low walls, through barely open gates and over advertising boards.

They flood on from the in-goal area, between the posts, from the half-way line, the 22s and 10-metre lines. They come from the Pwll End and the Town End, the North Enclosure and the South.

There are toothy girls, some clutching Cochyn cuddly toys, and gel-haired boys with great big grins. The backs of replica Scarlets shirts bear the names of Peel, B Davies, Jones, Easterby ... and Tom.

The Stradey Park pitch after the final whistle is awash with joy and delight, especially when the home team has won – as has just happened today. Winning's important to thousands here, but the experience is important too.

Only a few years ago hundreds scurried onto the pitch at half-time for a 10-minute dash with a rugby ball – but increasingly tight health and safety regulations put paid to that. However, the full-time ritual lives on. As the final whistle goes, the players of one

Home and away supporters, mascot Cochyn, Regan King and the traditional Scarlets v Bath rag doll trophy.

PLEASE KEEP OFF THE PITCH

team throw up their arms in delight, the losers bow their heads and slump their shoulders in dejection.

The kids catch them up, offer pats on back and begin the search for autographs.

The young sprinters are followed on more sedately by parents, grandparents, aunties and uncles. They face more of a challenge to clamber over and through the pitch-side obstacles.

Rugby balls fly into the air –there's even the occasional soccer ball. There are white rugby balls, yellow ones, big ones and small ones; there are sparkling new ones, grubby old ones, Gilbert, Reebok, KooGa, Mitre and Scarlets balls; there are Wales balls and Magners balls, performance varieties and bargain basket balls. There are kids tackling

kids, dads chasing kids, teenagers waving flags, mums teetering on heels, cuddling couples and babes in arms. It's like a human bagatelle; quick-witted youths pin-ball from one catch to another, young pals leap from one kick to the next. There are drop kicks, place kicks, up-and-unders and grubbers. Balls bobble across the turf like tumbleweed ripped up in a Mid West storm. Penalties and conversions are taken – balls sail over, under and wide of the crossbars.

At the entrance to the players' tunnel there's a scramble for signatures. Players sign programmes, tickets, magazines, autograph books, rugby balls, T-shirts, rugby shirts and flags. The kids love the clamour, the stewards look on with the players' well-being in mind and the players patiently and

diligently allow the supporters to have their piece of the action.

And then they're gone, children ushered away by parents, guardians and yellow-jacketed stewards. The groundsman has his turf back.

As the concrete of the stands and terracing reverts to its naked self, it's left with the temporary, human-inflicted scars of another battle.

There's the occasional cold chip and a latticework of French fries; redundant bread rolls await the big clean-up and there are legions of clear plastic pint pots marked "Magners." They're everywhere, from the walls of the enclosures to the steel framework of the Pwll End and the crush barriers of the Town End. They're in the footwells of the stands and on the steps on the terracing. Some stand upright, some are neatly stacked as if to suggest to disbelieving cleaners: "Your job's half done."

Hundreds more are lying side down being lolled gently by a breeze. Some leave a snail-trail of beer. Many have been crushed by the might of Timberland boots, Nike trainers and Matalan shoes – they lie cracked, splintered and crushed.

Some beer glasses have substantial remains of their pint, others just sticky smears of drink. Fellow fallen heroes include colourful drinks cans, squashed and buckled on the concrete. There's Pepsi, Fanta and numerous own-brand products.

Wounds have been inflicted on white polystyrene cups that once held milky tea, instant coffee or – maybe – hot chocolate.

Plastic drinks bottles reveal the strength and durability of today's throwaway packaging. Other than the loss of their tops, the Dr Pepper, Coke, Fanta, Sprite and 7-Up vessels remain remarkably intact, albeit rolling towards a concrete step or a red brick wall.

In the North Enclosure and the seating above, forlorn paper plates have been discarded, smeared and smudged in confectionary from a van in the Town End corner that specialises in "chocolate kebabs". Not so long ago the final-whistle terracing would have been speckled with fag ends – now the stadium's a no smoking zone.

This evening's detritus includes black A5 Magners promos for a texting competition called Time of the First Try – "When will the first try be scored in today's match? To win a signed shirt and a case of Magners pint bottles, text your name and answer to … "

There's the occasional worse-for-wear glossy programme ("Pop in with your programme and receive a 10% discount," advises Pizza Hut at Parc Trostre); there are match tickets and crumpled yellow 50-50 draw tickets ("Promoter DC Stroud, Assoc for the Development of Junior Rugby, Stradey Park. Winner receives 50% of net proceeds").

Scarlets staff such as head groundsman Dave Healey and caretaker Dai Jones prepare for more action. Part of their job is

The Haka, Llanelli style. Young supporters on the Stradey turf as part of pre-match entertainment in the build-up to October's victory over Ulster. Flags add to the spectacle.

The future is scarlet

Interviews
Ammanford RFC

MORE than 30 Scarlets players gather in a huddle under the blue skies of a chilly October morning. They're kitted out in co-ordinated KooGa sports gear – black short-sleeved training tops with narrow white hoops and red sleeves, dark shorts and dark socks. One player has skin-tight black athletic leggings.

Thickly-padded rucking shields in reds, yellows, black and blues are lined up behind a set of rugby posts.

Around the rugby posts are pads with the message: "Rugby@Roksport." Baskets of Maximuscle and Gilbert drinks bottles rest nearby.

There are kitbags, stacks of training cones and a cluster of rugby balls. The coaching staff, complete with physio Patrick Moran and fitness coach Wayne Proctor look on as the training session nears.

Clouds of white and grey begin to appear overhead as a breeze picks up behind the single-bar tubular steel fence around the pitch's perimeter. More Scarlets figures, in manager coats and tracksuit tops, mingle with around 200 schoolchildren behind the fence. The kids have already got posters carrying the Scarlets squad picture and most have signatures that the players patiently signed in a steady procession after arriving at the ground.

This is Ammanford RFC, and it's not the usual venue at which training is carried out – but it's one way in which Stradey Park is hooked in to the communities it serves. The event is a Scarlets On The Road training day, and the young guests are Stradey Park faithful of future years – or so the club hopes.

Jon Daniels, the club's head of community, says: "Training on the Road started last year and we're doing three of these sessions this year – this one, another in the Carmarthen area and one in Aberystwyth.

"It's a huge event for us as Scarlets because it means promoting rugby and

Young supporters during a Scarlets On The Road training day in Ammanford.

bringing youngsters closer to the club. It makes the squad more tangible and more real – they're no longer just a group of players seen on TV, at Stradey Park or at the Millennium Stadium.

"A lot of the squad were just the same as these children 20 years ago, a lot of them are from these areas, from the Gwendraeth Valley, from the Amman Valley, from Carmarthen – so hopefully it shows the young boys and girls here today that progression in rugby is achievable.

"By doing this we can make them realise that with talent, hard work and application, it's possible for them to become Scarlets players in the future."

So do the schoolkids appreciate the club's efforts?

Cerys Haf, aged 10, of Ysgol Gymraeg Rhydaman, says: "I've had autographs from players like Dwayne Peel and Stephen Jones.

I'm a Scarlets fan and it's nice to meet them – they're bigger than I expected."

School pal Serena Bethan, 10, says: "I'm not really a Scarlets fan – I'm an Ospreys fan. It's been different to meet the Scarlets players today. We've seen people like Dwayne Peel and they said: 'Hi, how are you?' I've got about 20 autographs on my team picture; I'm enjoying the day."

Friend Liam James, 10, says: "I'm a Scarlets fan and I've enjoyed meeting them – I've got autographs from people like Dwayne Peel and Stephen Jones. They're all much bigger than I'd expected – probably because they have to do lots of tackles."

Ysgol Gymraeg Rhydaman's Morgan Hill, 10, says: "I'm not really a big rugby fan but I follow the Scarlets and I enjoyed getting the autographs of people like Dwayne Peel. It's exciting to meet them and it's been different to a normal school day."

Ryan Lewis, 10, of Ysgol Penygroes, says: "I'm a Scarlets fan, big time – my favourites include Alix Popham and Simon Easterby and it's a great experience to meet them. Stradey Park's very old and has a lot of history and I've been to two games there. I've been in the changing rooms there but it's good to meet the players here."

School pal Mitchell Jones, 10, says: "I'm a big Scarlets fan – my heroes are Dwayne Peel, Stephen Jones and Regan King … oh, and Liam Davies. It's awesome to meet them close up – Stephen Jones told me that I could have his No 10 jersey in a few years because he'll be retired by the time I'm ready. I play for Penygroes and Dinefwr and District."

Joseph Davies, 10, of Ysgol Penygroes, says: "I play scrum-half for Penygroes and Dinefwr and District. Dwayne Peel and Liam Davies are my heroes and I've met them today. I said hello to them and it's amazing

to meet them – they're just as I expected; they're good. I've been to Stradey Park and it's awesome. I've been there for games and the atmosphere in the crowd is huge … awesome."

Kevin Davies, headteacher of Ysgol Penygroes, says: "It's important for a school like ours to come to an event like this because it's an opportunity for the children to meet their idols – a lot of them are Scarlets fans after all.

"We were part of a day out last Friday to see a match and a lot of the children hadn't been to a Stradey Park game before. It's particularly good for those children aspiring to be professional rugby players and it also has an important education quality – we were fortunate to have two of the Scarlets, Phil John and Deacon Manu, at school last week for a Q&A session. To prepare for that we collated 30 questions and

children typed them out – that was good for IT and English skills. Following that session, using the answers the players gave, we created player profiles for each one and did thank-you cards and letters – it's not just a one-off day, there's plenty of behind-the-scenes work and follow-up activity.

"To an extent we'll be able to take some of the training techniques back to school, and the Scarlets have also assigned a development officer to work with us for four or five weeks during school time.

"We've also got a little sports club and they've offered to come back for that too. It's important for children to see professional players and to understand that their lifestyles are different to those of most people because they've got to stick to strict diet and fitness regimes. The healthy lifestyles message fits in with an Assembly healthy schools

initiative. To fit in with that we've banned things like crisps from school. One of the questions to Phil John was: Do you eat five a day? The answer was that it was actually a lot more than that.

It seems that the Jon Daniel method of luring new fans in preparation for a new stadium is working. Slurping a welcome cuppa at pitchside in Ammanford, he says: "Some schools have already had rugby skills sessions, healthy lifestyle presentations with our healthy lifestyles partner and they've had Q&A sessions with our players … on subjects such as healthy eating.

"So this isn't a single hit – it's part of a sustained process and every child is given a complimentary Stradey Park ticket for themselves and an adult. Hopefully they'll come along, share in and contribute to the Stradey experience and come back in the future and become regulars.

"It really is the future, not just for developing players and encouraging children to play rugby but also encouraging the future of rugby in general – they might not be players but they might be coaches, first aiders, administrators, whatever. The important thing is that they become part of the wider rugby community in the future."

Meanwhile, the players break from their huddle and fitness man Wayne Proctor says: "Let's go, gentlemen, please!"

And they're off jogging … dipping under a fence's handrail to test their flexibility. It's only a little stoop for 5ft 11in Dwayne Peel but a less graceful full body tuck for 6ft 4in Simon Easterby.

They return in small groups, chipping and catching a ball. Children in school uniform, Scarlets tops and warm coats look on with interest.

The players progress through an hour of ball handling, stretching, eight-a-side touch rugby and passing moves from a make-believe breakdown area through the backs to the wingers. After every couple of moves there's a discussion with coaches Phil Davies, Paul Moriarty and Robert Jones. There's line-out practice and scrummaging.

The children shout "Scarlets!" and "Oggy oggy oggy!"

A capacity crowd enjoys some floodlit action with the Ospreys.

The 2007-08 season saw Wales win
the RBS Six Nations Grand Slam.
Their trophy and Triple Crown shield
made a special visit to Stradey Park.

Three songs

With thanks to Mary Ann, Dafydd & Max

Two songs represented the sound of Stradey as it entered its final days — the traditional Sosban Fach and Dafydd Iwan's Yma o Hyd. The former was still sung by sections of the crowd during games, and a snippet of a modern dance music mix was played after a conversion by the home team. Tries and successful penalty kicks were followed by a thumping blast of the Yma o Hyd chorus.

Another song, by entertainer Max Boyce, may not have been heard on the stands and terraces but it captures beautifully the excitement of one big day at the ground. It's called 9-3.

Sosban Fach

Mae bys Mary-Ann wedi brifo
A Dafydd y gwas ddim yn iach
Mae'r baban yn y crub yn crio
A'r gath wedi sgrapo Jonni bach.
Sosban fach yn berwi ar y tan,
Sosban fawr yn berwi ar y llawr,
A'r gath wedi sgrapo Jonni bach.
Dai bach yn soldiwr,
Dai bach yn soldiwr,
Dai bach yn soldiwr,
A gwt ei grys e mas.
Mae bys Mary-Ann wedi gwella
A Dafydd y gwas yn ei fedd
Mae'r baban yn y cryb yn ddistaw
A'r gath nawr yn cysgu mewn hedd.
Sosban fach yn berwi ar y tan,
Sosban fawr yn berwi ar y llawr,
A'r gath nawr yn cysgu mewn hedd.

Little Saucepan

Mary-Ann has hurt her finger,
And Dafydd the servant is not well.
The baby in the cradle is crying,
And the cat has scratched little Johnny.
A little saucepan is boiling on the fire,
A big saucepan is boiling on the floor,
And the cat has scratched little Johnny.
Little Dai is a soldier,
Little Dai is a soldier,
Little Dai is a soldier,
And his shirt tail is hanging out.
Mary-Ann's finger has got better,
And Dafydd the servant is in his grave;
The baby in the cradle has grown up,
And the cat is asleep in peace.
A little saucepan is boiling on the fire,
A big saucepan is boiling on the floor,
And the cat has scratched little Johnny.

Words from www.sing4wales.com

9-3

It was on a dark and dismal day
In a week that had seen rain,
When all roads led to Stradey Park
With the All Blacks here again.
They poured down from the valleys,
They came from far and wide;
There were twenty-thousand in the ground
And me and Dai outside!

The shops were closed like Sunday,
And the streets were silent still.
And those who chose to stay away
Were either dead or ill.

But those who went to Stradey, boys,
Will remember till they die
How New Zealand were defeated,
And how the pubs ran dry.

Oh, the beer flowed at Stradey
(Piped down from Felinfoel),
And the hands that held the glasses high
Were strong from steel and coal.
And the air was filled with singing,
And I saw a grown man cry.
Not because we'd won
But because the pubs ran dry!

Yma o Hyd

	We're Still Here!
Dwyt ti'm yn cofio Macsen	You don't remember Macsen
Does neb yn ei nabod o	Who was he, you don't know?
Mae mil a chwe chant o flynyddoedd	One thousand and six hundred years
Yn amser rhy hir i'r co'	Is far, far too long ago.
Aeth Magnus Maximus o Gymru	When Magnus Maximus left Wales
Yn y flwyddyn tri chant wyth tri	Three eighty three was the year,
A'n gadael yn genedl gyfan	He left us as a whole nation
A heddiw – wele ni!	And today – look, we're still here!
Ryn ni yma o hyd!	We're still here today!
Ryn ni yma o hyd!	We're still here today
Er gwaetha pawb a phopeth	Despite everything and everyone
Er gwaetha pawb a phopeth	Despite everything and everyone
Er gwaetha pawb a phopeth	Despite everything and everyone
Ryn ni yma o hyd!	We're still here today.
Chwythed y gwynt o'r Dwyrain	Let the wind blow from the East
Rhued y storm o'r môr	Let the storm from the sea roar,
Hollted y mellt yr wybren	Let the sky split with lightning
A gwaedded y daran encôr	Let thunderbolts shout encore.
Llifed dagrau'r gwangalon	Let the fainthearted keep wailing
A llyfed y taeog y llawr	Let the serfs grovel and fawn,
Er dued y fagddu o'n cwmpas	In spite of the darkness around us
Ry'n ni'n barod am doriad y wawr!	We're ready to greet a new dawn.
Cofiwn i Facsen Wledig	Remember that old Prince Macsen
Adael ein gwlad yn un darn	He left our country as one,
A bloeddiwn gerbron y gwledydd	Let's shout out to all the nations
'Mi fyddwn yma tan Ddydd y Farn!'	'We'll be here until kingdom come!'
Er gwaetha pob Dic Siôn Dafydd	Despite all the collaborators,
Er gwaetha'r "Hen Elyn" a'i chriw	Despite "the Old Enemy", we're alive,
Byddwn yma hyd ddiwedd amser	We'll be here for ever and ever
A bydd yr iaith Gymraeg yn fyw!	The Welsh language will survive!

Words by Dafydd Iwan, copyright Cyhoeddiadau Sain

Then dawned the morning after
On empty factories.
But we were still at Stradey –
Bloodshot absentees.
But we all had doctors' papers
And they all said just the same:
That we all had Scarlet Fever,
And we caught it at the game!

Now all the little babies
In Llanelli from now on
Will be christened Ray or Carwyn,
Derek, Delme, Phil or John.

And in a hundred years again
They'll sing this song for me
Of when the scoreboard read "Llanelli 9,
Seland Newydd 3."

And when I'm old and my hair turns grey
And they put me in a chair,
I'll tell my great-grandchildren
That their Datcu was there.
And they'll ask to hear the story
Of that damp October day,
When I went down to Stradey
And I saw the Scarlets play.

*Words by Max Boyce,
copyright Max Boyce*

SCARLETS

Heroes,
one and all

Neither the players, coaching staff nor water carriers were going to take this one sitting down. One of Welsh rugby's great traditional rivalries – Llanelli RFC v Pontypridd RFC – ended 13-13 in October 2007. This was the home dugout.

On cold days kick off with Bovril

Interview
Handel Greville

MEMORABLE rugby dinners don't come much more star studded than an extravaganza held on the Millennium Stadium pitch just before Christmas 2005.

In a huge marquee, more than 150 former Welsh internationals were among around 1,000 guests who had gathered to mark 125 years of the Welsh Rugby Union.

Diners included John Taylor, Graham Price, JJ Williams and Clive Rowlands. There was David Watkins, Gareth Edwards, John Dawes, Phil Bennett, Gerald Davies, JPR Williams, Jonathan Davies and Ieuan Evans.

The oldest cap present was 85-year-old ex-Cardiff centre Jack Matthews. Former Llanelli wing Peter Rees was another man there to have hit his 80s, along with an 84-year-old whose only Wales appearance had come almost five decades earlier.

Handel Greville had been Llanelli scrum-half when he'd helped Wales beat Australia 6-0 at Cardiff in December 1947. The matchday programme's cover that day had featured two advertisements – "On cold days kick off with Bovril" and "Mitchells & Butlers good honest beer."

Now it's late 2007 and a modest framed photo of the 26-year-old Handel – in Wales jersey and cap – now hangs in the tidy front room of his bungalow in Drefach, high in the majestic Gwendraeth Valley.

Handel, born a miner's son in Drefach in 1921, admits that memories of his playing days are a little more vague than they once were.

However, Stradey will never leave his heart. His father Arthur, who played three games for Llanelli, took him as a schoolboy on treasured trips to the ground in the 1930s.

He says: "My dad would take me to watch games there, and it was quite an experience. We'd go down by bus, get dropped off in

129

town and walk down towards Stradey.

"There were no entertaining facilities at the ground so the players would meet at the old Salutation pub, close to where today's library stands. They'd walk to Stradey for the game and, as boys, we'd watch for them coming out and would carry their bags to the ground.

"I can't recall if we were given anything for doing this but that wouldn't have mattered; we were just proud to have carried the bag of Ivor Jones or Dai John.

"Traffic wasn't as it is now – there might have been the odd car or a bike. You could walk untroubled, and it was a great pleasure to rub shoulders with these Llanelli players – it meant a lot to me as a schoolboy.

"At the ground, we wouldn't sit in Stradey's single stand, I suppose my dad couldn't afford it. There was a terrace in front where we'd stand.

"Another difference today's crowds would notice would be that there were no women in the crowd – rugby was a man thing then."

Handel developed into a useful schoolboy player, representing the old Gwendraeth Grammar School and the Mynydd Mawr representative side.

Before he could graduate to senior rugby, war broke out. Teenage Handel was posted to Egypt with the RAF and only returned in 1946. Back home, he played a game for Tumble and was immediately picked up by Llanelli. Mod cons were in short supply for Stradey Park's players.

Handel says: "The accommodation was primitive. The changing rooms had a communal bath made of concrete; it was filthy, it wasn't plastered or tiled.

"We'd jump into the bath quickly before anybody else because that's when the water would be clean. It was very unhygienic."

"At the time we took it for granted. A lot of houses at that time didn't have washing facilities – miners would get home and wash in a zinc bath. We didn't know anything better."

The players of the day also had concerns other than the game.

Handel recalls: "Our teams included men from the steelworks; they'd go straight from the works to train – they wouldn't even have chance to change."

The opponents were often different to today as well.

Handel says: "During the time I was involved with the club there were 16 clubs playing first class rugby in Wales. The Western Mail was very much involved with an unofficial championship and it was a great honour to be up there near the top.

"Now, of course, the focus is very much on the four regions – but we'd regularly play great English teams like Leicester, Northampton and the London clubs. I used to like playing them because it was easy, we'd beat them with little trouble.

"I much preferred playing the English rather than teams like Aberavon or Neath. I don't think the English took it as seriously as we did – they certainly weren't as aggressive."

Handel ended his senior rugby days with Swansea but stayed on at Stradey on the administrative side.

Scarlets players hard at work during a 2007-08 training session.

He became chairman and president of the Llanelli club and helped bring about some important changes to the ground.

He says: "During this period Llanelli RFC bought Stradey from Mr Mansel-Lewis to begin developing it gradually."

New terracing, stands, admin areas and entertainment facilities followed.

Now Handel will be sad to leave – but he pledges to keep a close eye on what's going on and intends to keep fit through sport.

He smiles: "I keep active by playing golf at Ashburnham – my standard's pretty low, mind, but I only started playing in the early 1970s; my handicap's never been below 16."

It might be interesting to speculate on how much more recognised he could have been as a rugby player had World War Two been avoided.

Yet he's not one to linger on possible negatives. In fact, the hostilities opened new doors.

He says: "I was sent to Cairo and played for the RAF out there. I had a wonderful time playing rugby there – I remember a tournament between the RAF and the Army, and international games when the Welsh played the English; we had a lot of fun.

"We got to play against men who were internationals and it was a great privilege for me to be playing against people such as Les Mansfield, a Welsh international, and Tommy Kemp, an England fly-half."

We were born among heroes

Interviews
Past players

THE Scarlets Past Players Association continues to keep the memories alive. And today, in November 2007, they have arranged a Stradey Park get together for one final team picture at the ground they once graced as players.

Around 100 of them turn up, representing seven decades of Llanelli rugby history. There's a lot of chatting to be done as individuals born as far back as the 1920s mingle with recent stars such as Ieuan Evans and Rupert Moon.

They talk about big games and forgotten games, families, friends, workmates and clubmates. There are lots of smiles – and not just for the camera.

Wyn Lloyd played on the wing for Llanelli in the 1940s.

Aged 82, he says: "I was brought up in Furnace and worked in a nearby engineering works. Stradey is a home from home. To play for the Scarlets was a thrill – I didn't play many games, I just had a walk-on part, really."

Aubrey Gale played for the club in the 1950s and 1960s.

He says: "I'm Stradey born and bred, spending many hours as a boy playing rugby, cricket, soccer and many other things down here. I lived outside the ground for the biggest part of my life, particularly when I was playing."

Ray Williams played as a back for Llanelli from 1946 to 1961 and for Wales.

As a schoolteacher his pupils included Barry John.

Ray still lives in Hedley Terrace, Llanelli. He says: "To us Stradey Park is a kind of Mecca. I played my first game here in 1946 but I can just about go back to 1935 when me and my father watched Jack Manchester's New Zealand All Blacks here. Can you imagine the affect that had on a young Welsh

speaking boy from Felinfoel Primary School?

"In World War Two I was called up just before the end of hostilities and I was lucky enough to play for my village side on a weekend pass. I was then asked to play for Llanelli the following night. Strangely enough, although I was thrilled, we'd had five and a half years of war and upheaval so it wasn't the be all and end all.

"I had two and half years away with the Forces so on getting back there was the serious business of having to prove myself. It was a challenge – play well for Felinfoel and then get back in at Stradey.

"In the early 1950s, the ground had a

railing all the way around it, with spikes sticking up. The Tanner Bank was made of ash from the local steelworks, and – although the club wasn't doing particularly well – the feeling just got into you; it got into your blood, it wasn't just a game, it was a way of life.

"Rugby was an amateur sport, of course, not all that well organised but we just got on with it.

"After training on Thursdays the boys would have a couple of pints but that was it – stop. So we could be at our reasonable best on the Saturday afternoon none of us would go to the pub on the Friday night.

"There were so few other attractions – radio yes but television hadn't reared its ugly head – that it was something to get your name in the newspaper. I was lucky to play through the 50s with all the talent that was here then – and we still keep in touch because it's the people that make Stradey; the ground is a patch of green with goalposts but it's the people, the attitudes that make it."

Doug Williams played for Llanelli in the early 1950s and is now secretary of the past players association.

After the commemorative photograph is taken in the North Stand, he says: "I was born and raised in the shadow of the Town End goalposts, I played here as a boy and during the war helped to mark the pitch.

"Us local boys used half the pitch as our own ground. I lived in Derwent Street and my brother Ossie went on to play for Llanelli and Wales. Other relatives played too and Stradey now has so much tradition.

"I remember there being no North Stand, just the Tanner Bank.

"As boys, when we couldn't afford to pay to get in, we'd climb over the wall or we'd watch for the players to carry their bags through the gates so we wouldn't have to pay. We were born amongst heroes and we lived as heroes."

Around 100 members of the Scarlets Past Players Association during a get-together for a special photo. Between them they represent more than seven decades of Llanelli rugby history.

Steve & Rob stay strong

Interviews
Stephen Jones and Robin McBryde

ROBIN McBryde and Stephen Jones are hunched at separate tables, with queues snaking back from each.

The star duo – one a former Stradey Park hero, one still very much part of the Scarlets – each have a pen.

On request from those heading the queues they craft a short message and a signature in paperback books. It's all done with a smile, a laugh and a click of the mobile phone camera.

It's December 2007 in the Tetley's Suite and personnel from West Wales publisher Y Lolfa are hosting an event to launch three books – Staying Strong by McBryde, the Welsh language O Clermont I Nantes by Jones and John Hefin's Grand Slam: Behind the Scenes of the Classic Film.

The event is being compered by Alun Wyn Bevan, the author of another popular rugby–related book, Stradey Stories.

He tells the 200 supporters here tonight: "There are some individuals from North Wales who've managed to create an impression on rugby's international scene – people such as Tony Grey, Arthur Emyr, Andy Moore and Steve Moore.

"They played for Wales and won a handful of caps, but Robin McBryde went on to represent his country on many, many occasions. The mental toughness, the attitude, the personality which is part of Stephen's being as well is also truly represented by Robin McBryde. He has now become a coach and will succeed in that role. Robin and Stephen are great players, but more importantly they're great individuals and great men."

Down the years books have had an important part to play in the evolution of Stradey Park's heritage. They range from the anecdotal to the more scholarly breed.

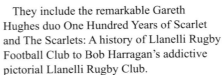

They include the remarkable Gareth Hughes duo One Hundred Years of Scarlet and The Scarlets: A history of Llanelli Rugby Football Club to Bob Harragan's addictive pictorial Llanelli Rugby Club.

McBryde's new tome features lively tales from his rugby career. The Jones paperback describes the outside-half's experiences from September 2006 through to his part in Wales' dramatic Rugby World Cup defeat against Fiji in France just over a year later.

After two hours of chat, questions and answers and signing books the players sit at a quiet table to talk about Stradey Park and its imminent closure. McBryde says: "Th where everything came true for me – out the park. This is where I've enjoyed most my experiences playing for the Scarlets, tasting success in cup and league. The experiences we had in Europe were brilli

"The one man who sums it all up is Gra He took Llanelli with him wherever he w He was a great ambassador for the club a our involvement with the club together meant a lot to me. Recently, when he had amputation of his leg, I stood in for him o

A 2007 book launch in the Tetley's Suite.

sword-bearing duties at the Eisteddfod. Gravs was Gravs – it didn't matter where you bumped into him he'd always leave you with a smile on your face. He was a huge character and will be a great loss.

"The funeral here was a unique day as Gravs was a unique man. There were fears that it might turn into a circus, that it might go a bit over the top but I think those responsible for organising it showed that we can hold things like that in Wales brilliantly. There was nothing false about it, nothing pretentious and everything was done spot-on.

"I think the day, certainly for those who

attended and watched it on television, had the ability to touch everybody. I was so glad and honoured to have played a part in it. It was an honour to have the sword in that setting – indeed, Gravs had spoken tongue in cheek about me being the Eisteddfod sword bearer after him, so it was ironic that I performed that very duty on his day."

Jones says: "Stradey Park is a very special place for me – it's where I started my rugby career at a senior level. I've been fortunate to play here since 1996 and have had so many wonderful rugby moments out there on that

pitch that I've developed a big emotional attachment.

"Some games have been very special, especially those in Heineken Cup campaigns. It's a great place to play – there's passionate support, the supporters are close to the pitch and the atmosphere's always outstanding.

"It's hard to pinpoint one particular high – although the 24-12 victory over Leicester in 2002 was massive. They were such a dominant force at the time, with the majority of the Leicester side in the England squad that was dominating the Six Nations."

Hard knocks
with my heroes

Interview
Derek Quinnell

WITH the glory comes the grime. Just ask Derek Quinnell. The Llanelli and Lions hero knows all too well that to enjoy the pleasure you've first got to experience the pain.

As a teenager in the Stradey Park youth teams of the mid-1960s, he would sometimes train with the seniors. The experience stood him in good stead.

Now a businessman based in Llanelli's North Dock, he looks back with a wry smile. He says: "Occasionally we were invited to train with the Scarlets. They thought I had some potential so I'd train with Llanelli on the Monday, the youth on a Tuesday, Llanelli on a Wednesday and the youth on the Thursday. I'd have Friday off then play a game on the Saturday. That was the time at Stradey that I enjoyed the most – I was a young guy training with my heroes and on Saturdays we'd play a youth game, get changed quickly and watch the Scarlets play.

"My heroes included Norman and Byron Gale. By then Norman had captained Wales against New Zealand. Delme Thomas was a hero. He'd been on the 1966 Lions tour and, as an 18-year-old in youth rugby, I played in the second row at Stradey with Delme – it doesn't get any better than that.

"In the Youth we all aspired to get into the senior team to rub shoulders with guys we thought were fantastic. Hoping to rub shoulders with these guys and, perhaps, having the odd game meant it was a fantastic time for me.

"All those figures were inspirational – people like Joe Leleu and Marlston Morgan. We trained with them and they were tough cookies. Quite often they'd use us as a bit of a doormat in training sessions and we'd come off with bloodied noses. It taught us to grow up a little bit and helped us develop from youths into men. It certainly helped my development pretty quickly. They were a hard school and recognised that I needed

toughening up. They were passionate about the game but caring as well – when they knocked you down they picked you up again."

Talking about Stradey Park in October 2007, Quinnell says: "I was born in Llanelli and moved for a short while to Trimsaran. My first visit to the ground was with my grandfather, Wyndham Nurse, when I was about 12 in the early 1960s. He took us on a bus to see a floodlit game.

"I forget who the opponents were on that first occasion and who was kicking for Llanelli but somebody took a shot at goal from a long way out and hit the crossbar. It came back and I turned to my grandfather

to say: 'Ooh, almost made it' – but before I could turn back Ray Williams, who was playing wing for Llanelli, had followed up, caught the bounce off the floor and scored under the posts. It was the only try that night and I missed it. However, Llanelli won the game and I came away well satisfied. Before getting back on the bus to get home I had a bag of chips – it was a great night out. Since then I've always thought there was something romantic about floodlit games, especially those on cold wintry nights standing on the Tanner Bank."

Quinnell's grandfather, born in 1900, was a great scholar of the game and took great

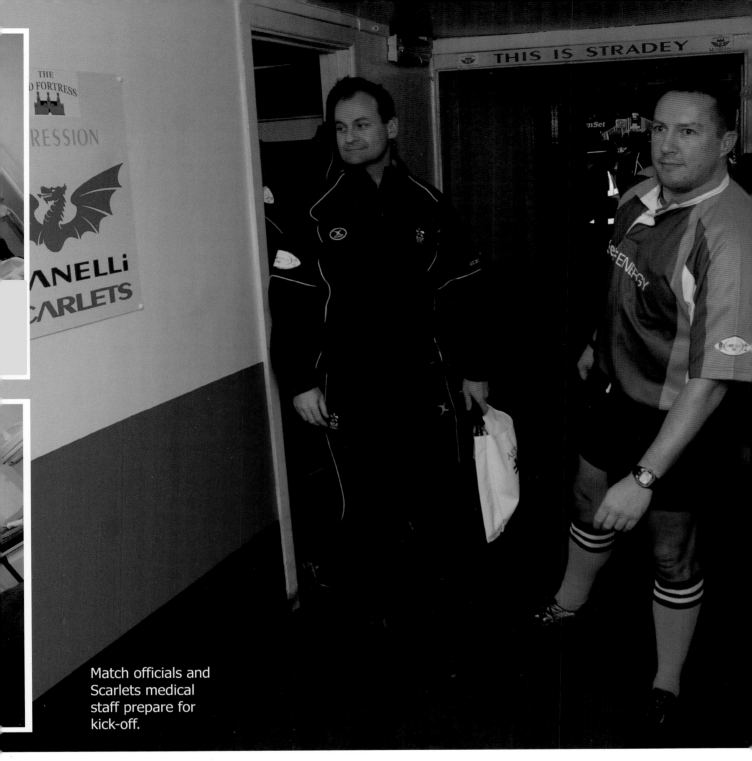

THIS IS STRADEY

Match officials and
Scarlets medical
staff prepare for
kick-off.

pride in the fact that Derek and his sons went on to play for Llanelli.

Early recollections of the Stradey flair didn't end with the great Ray Williams. Quinnell says: "I remember being in Coleshill Secondary Modern School and playing rugby with Phil Bennett. He was in the same school year as me and we won the under-15 Welsh sevens which was quite a prestigious competition. I thought that would be the pinnacle of my career – although we also played a few games together for Llanelli Schoolboys at Stradey and that was terrific.

"Phil was a fantastic player. As schoolboys we knew that if we won enough ball and gave him some space he'd do something special for us. I was fortunate to go on and play most of my rugby with Benny and it was always my job to simply get the ball – unfortunately for him it was his job to do the rest. This wasn't always easy but he usually did it."

Playing together at Stradey Park through Llanelli RFC's 1970s golden era, things were frequently enthralling.

Quinnell says: "There was something special about playing Floodlight Alliance games. It might have only lasted five years or so but Llanelli always seemed to enjoy it. The scoring was done on tries only – no kicks, no penalties, no conversions – and this suited our brand of football because that's the way we played.

"However, when there was a glut of games at Stradey it wasn't the greatest place to play. I remember one Christmas playing London Welsh on Boxing Day and Bristol the following day, a Friday and Saturday. There'd be 20,000-plus people there for London Welsh and a lot for Bristol too.

"We played Bristol on a quagmire because it had been wet the previous day and the pitch had cut up badly. It was sticky mud against Bristol and I wish I had a recording of that game because somehow we played

Scarlets heroes Simon Easterby, Dafydd Jones and Deacon Manu prepare for action in the home dressing room.

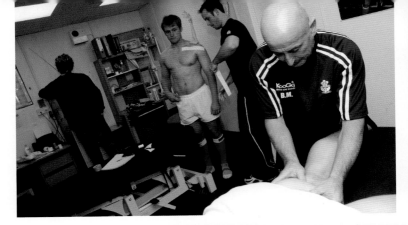

some magnificent rugby football and scored 50 points."

Bennett wasn't the only talented Scarlets star of that era. Quinnell says: "If you compare the 1969-70 side that played the Springboks to the side that beat the All Blacks in 1972 you'll see only a couple of players who played in both games.

"That's because we had a lot of young talent coming through.

"Ieuan Evans had been the coach when I arrived – he was also coach of the Welsh Youth and he bought the best to Stradey, most of them West Walian as it happened. Carwyn James succeeded him and brought in players like JJ Williams, Chico Hopkins and Tom David.

"For the All Blacks, Ray Gravell, Roy Bergiers, JJ, Andy Hill, Roger Davies, Barry Llewelyn and Tony Crocker were all there.

"It was an exciting time to be around and the majority of that side took us through the 70s which was a great period for Llanelli and Wales.

"When we played, fortunately, rugby wasn't our job – it was our hobby. We enjoyed it, turned up twice a week for training and on Saturday for the game and had a few pints together. Most of us started work at 8am finished at 5pm and drove to training.

"A lot of us did that for a long period and it involved weekend trips to places like London, Leicester and Coventry.

"Something suffered and that was normally the families – the wives and children suffered for having the honour of dad playing for Llanelli. However, the wives and girlfriends did come to home games and enjoyed themselves – the club looked after us reasonably well in that respect."

Now, although the Scarlets and Llanelli RFC will continue to visit the big names in rugby union, there will no longer be reciprocal occasions for Stradey Park.

Quinnell says: "Big clubs like Wasps, Leicester and Gloucester always enjoyed coming to Stradey.

"It was great playing there every week so you get used to the slope on the pitch. Guys making their first visit would often say: Christ, we're playing uphill in both halves!"

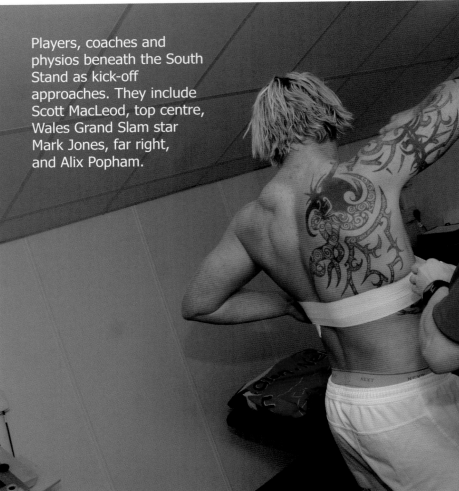

Players, coaches and physios beneath the South Stand as kick-off approaches. They include Scott MacLeod, top centre, Wales Grand Slam star Mark Jones, far right, and Alix Popham.

Thoroughbreds down the pub

Interview
Sean Gale

IT came as no surprise to Norman Gale that son Sean became part of Llanelli rugby history.

Dad had skippered Wales in the late 1960s as he built a solid reputation at hooker for Llanelli.

He died in 2005 at the age of 65 – but by then he knew that his family would be always linked with Stradey Park. His former

role as landlord of a pub close to the ground helped.

Enjoying a morning off work at home in Swiss Valley in October 2007 Sean says: "The White Horse is a stone's throw from Stradey so, as I was growing up there, all the older players like Stuart Gallacher would show up. I knew all the players – all the great stars. People like Ray Gravell would be there regularly; he was almost part of the furniture."

Indeed, Gravell said of Norman Gale in 2005: "He played a huge part in the success of Llanelli RFC as a player and administrator. He was a hard man and a passionate man who loved and understood his rugby."

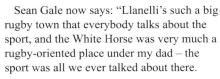

Sean Gale now says: "Llanelli's such a big rugby town that everybody talks about the sport, and the White Horse was very much a rugby-oriented place under my dad – the sport was all we ever talked about there.

"In the early 80s, when I was 14 or 15, pub opening times were much more limited than they are today so things could get hectic. Six or seven times every season the visiting team would be traditional Welsh rivals Swansea, Neath or Pontypridd and supporters would be knocking the pub open at 11am. By noon they'd be six deep at the bar and, as the minutes ticked by, it got to the point where you couldn't move.

"There'd regularly be crowds of 15,000 – there was less to do in those days so people would be much more inclined to treat a rugby match as a day out."

As a young schoolboy, Sean became a Stradey Park ballboy and soon began operating the scoreboard. He became increasingly determined to play for Llanelli.

He played for the under-15s, under-16s and Llanelli Youth and won a Welsh Schools cap. At 18 he went on a Llanelli tour of Australia.

He says: "We had some colourful fixtures over the years, some real hidings and some great joy.

"One great memory I have is of the All Blacks at Stradey in 1989 – it was a horrible night but it was full to the rafters and there was a unique atmosphere, the best atmosphere I can remember. It was great to be there and sing the anthems – great."

Once his playing days ended, Sean strengthened his Stradey links, coaching with Scott Quinnell and Neil Boobyer.

He says: "My father was a player, captain, assistant coach, head coach, club chairman and chairman of the past players association. He was involved in some capacity for 80% of his life – so Stradey was bred into me.

"Stradey Park was an everyday occurrence for me; I'd go there for every little thing. The ground has been with me my whole life – I've got a lot of great memories and I've made a lot of good friends there. I've thoroughly enjoyed being a small part of its history and I'll certainly miss it when it goes, but exciting times lie ahead."

'We only loaned him!'

**Interviews
Paul John
and Wayne Cullen**

PONTYPRIDD is one of Welsh rugby's great names. The club will always be given a warm welcome by Llanelli RFC.

Formed in 1876, Ponty can list among its former stars one Tommy David. In 1967, he made the first of 404 appearances for the club.

The club's website reports: "Although we loaned him to Llanelli for a couple of seasons so that they could beat the All Blacks, he was back at Pontypridd and in the Welsh team for the centenary season in 1975-76."

The 1975-81 period was a golden era for Ponty, winning the Western Mail championship three times, winning the Merit Table competition once and reaching the WRU Cup final for the first time in 1979. The Australian touring team played at Sardis Road in 1981, winning a titanic struggle just 6-3.

There was a first Welsh Cup win in 1996, narrow defeat to South Africa, European competition and a league championship in 1997.

Capped stars in recent decades have included Dale "The Chief" McIntosh, Neil Jenkins, Richie Collins, Paul John, Martyn Williams, Gareth Wyatt, Dafydd James, Mike Griffiths and Ian Gough. Michael Owen, Robert Sidoli, Mefin Davies, Gethin Jenkins, Sonny Parker, Jonny Bryant and Ceri Sweeney were among those to follow.

In 2003 Ponty joined with Bridgend to form ill-fated regional outfit the Celtic Warriors, with the club side entering the new semi-pro Welsh Premier Division. Pontypridd are now linked to regional side the Cardiff Blues and, after financial difficulties, are back on an even keel.

A 2005 Konica Minolta Cup final appearance ended in defeat to Llanelli – but the following year they lifted the trophy, beating Neath.

Piling in during a Llanelli v Pontypridd club game.

Their home grounds have included some evocative rugby names – Ynysangharad and Trallwn Fields, Taff Vale and People's Park. Since 1974 they've played at Sardis Road, developed in a former colliery area known locally as Dan's Muck Hole.

Such history means a lasting affinity between Ponty and Llanelli – even as the visitors leave Stradey Park with a hint of disappointment on October 27, 2007. A 13-13 draw could well have gone the visitors' way – but there were no fall-outs.

After the post-match press conference, Ponty coach Paul John, a capped scrum-half who retired from playing two years ago, says: "As a player there's one time I'll never forget here. It was a night in the early 90s when Llanelli secured the double.

"Stradey Park was packed and, in typical Stradey style, the supporters had their victory T-shirts printed before they'd even won. We played really well but still ended up losing by 40-odd points. Llanelli had a phenomenal team, with people like Mark Perego, and I seem to remember ending up at outside-half, with No 10 Neil Jenkins ending up at centre – we were down to the bare bones. It's always a difficult place to come and win."

John smiles: "The supporters here are one-eyed, there's no about it; I sat in the stand today laughing at some of the things they were saying.

"I've always enjoyed coming down here, we even won on a few occasions and that was a great achievement.

"The place has so much unbelievable history and heritage that it's a pity the ground must go – but in this era it all comes down to money, and they need a new ground."

On his way from changing room to Tetley's Suite dinner, Ponty team manager Wayne Cullen – who enjoyed a 38-year career with the Army – says: "Visiting Stradey Park is always a great occasion; it's got a great rugby history and Llanelli-Ponty is always a wonderfully hard South v West match.

"The ground and its facilities are superb and hopefully they'll be replicated when the club moves.

"My memories include so many games here that have been extremely tight and they include recollections of great players who've run out onto this park. I'll also always remember the hospitality that's shown to us when we come here – it's superb."

Wayne's memories go back some time.

He says: "I think the first time I came here was a long, long time ago, in schools rugby at the age of around 12. Through the years I've been here at different stages in my rugby.

"I played here for the Army against the famous Llanelli side of the Phil Bennett era – I played here two or three times on a Friday night of an international weekend.

"The Ponty-Llanelli rivalry has been a superb, friendly rivalry for an enormous length of time. Something might be lost with the move from Stradey Park – but I'm sure the club will take the spirit with them."

Bert, the rub-a-dub man

Interview
Laurance Delaney

CHANGING room characters can be crucial to success – even when they don't have a direct influence on tactics. Take Bert Peel. Former Wales cap Laurance Delaney remembers him well.

"He was our rub-a-dub man – our physio," says Laurance from the comfort of a front room armchair at home in Saron. "He had a little room at Stradey, on the left as you go out of the players' tunnel, and he'd only let one or two of us in at any one time. He'd get through us all eventually.

"He was such a humorous character, he had loads of stories and, as a young man before a game, this would relax you even though he only had the one couch – there wasn't room for any more. You'd queue up to go in there and just hear him shout: 'Next!' You'd open the door and the couch would be right in front of you. He'd warm you up, strap a leg maybe, or rub in horse liniment.

"Other than the couch, his only equipment would be a single heat lamp and an ultrasound machine. This was a little box of tricks – his little toy; he'd put it on you for anything – even if you didn't have a bad leg. He'd be talking away whilst prodding with this ultrasound."

Delaney, a prop who played 501 games for Llanelli in the 1970s, 1980s and 1990s, says: "Bert wore tracksuit bottoms that looked like ballerina trousers and a T-shirt pulled over his plump upper body – he looked quite a figure.

"On the bus he was good company too – he'd come up with a different story every trip. And Bert, of course, was the man who'd run on the field to tend to an injured player. He was a real one-man band, with his magic sponge. In fact, he'd just talk you out of an injury using psychology – he'd say: 'Oh, there's nothing wrong with you – just carry on.' He was one of those characters, a real important part of the changing room – he'd keep us going, no trouble."

Delaney, born in 1956, says in October 2007 that his earliest memories of Stradey Park are from his schoolboy days when he stood on the Tanner Bank. He says: "We'd be excited at going down to Stradey and then waiting for half-time when we could run on the field to try to meet the players and get some autographs. There'd also be the temptation of a half-time hot dog with onions – the van would be down by today's medical centre. You'd have enough money to pay to get in and buy a hot dog and that was it.

"We'd try to sit on the field, making arrangements in school to try to meet at the best place, normally the half-way line. You'd always have the same people around you and you'd get to know them – some lived by you, others elsewhere. It was a very appealing experience, with an adrenaline rush as you

got involved in the game. In these days there were a lot of staunch Llanelli people, the Tanner Bank would be full. At the end of the game many of the crowd wouldn't leave straight away; they'd wait for other scores to be announced. It was great – none of this leaving before the final whistle."

As a teenager the passion grew. Laurance says: "I was lucky enough to be there when we beat the All Blacks in 1972. It was a very exciting day and I was just at the age where you'd sneak into the pubs for an under-age drink – I have fond memories of that day.

"From that era I remember some of the Tanner Bank characters who'd get a sing-song going. One character was Ray the Cat – his incredible voice would stick out above the crowd. He was comical, he'd get the crowd going and give the referees some

It's gametime. The North Stand is busy, the Scarlets bench is animated and the Llanelli RFC changing room is all-action even at half-time.

stick. We used to laugh with such people – it was an important part of our growing up.

"My ambition when I went to Stradey in those days was driven by ego – I wanted to play for Llanelli. I was lucky enough to do that eventually and I well remember games in the Floodlight Alliance."

As a pupil of Stebonheath Secondary Modern School, Laurance played for Llanelli Schoolboys for a few years and was given the chance to play at Stradey Park.

He says: "The first time I played there would've been when I was 14 or 15. It was out of this world – we couldn't wait to get into the changing room to see what was there. We walked in past the away dressing room then we'd see the sign that said 'Home dressing room.' We'd go in and

imagine the famous people who'd been in that room – we'd all be excited, all 15 of us.

"More often, Llanelli Schoolboys would play at Stradey School and I remember that after a game we'd go into the canteen and they'd have these big old fashioned stainless steel trays piled high with beans and chips."

After leaving school, Laurance played for local club New Dock Stars but eventually joined Llanelli where one memorable figure remained. Laurance says: "I put on the red jersey and ran out with the stars on Stradey Park, a cauldron with the big crowds, a full Tanner Bank … and Ray the Cat! The fans called me Bully and individuals would shout: 'Go on Bully, show him the way!' I'd be laughing inside but it did used to drive you on. I loved listening to the Tanner Bank which was where the real working class

figures would be, the steelworkers, the coal workers – those people loved their rugby and their comments would spur us on because they created such an atmosphere. Having a big crowd behind you like that was worth a few points."

There were a number of big occasions when the crowd really did lift Llanelli to victory.

Laurance says: "There was one time in 1985 when we were playing Fiji and we were down 25-0 before half-time. After half-time the crowd really got behind us, we scored a try early on and we ended up winning 31-28. The best atmosphere I experienced as a player was in 1992 when we beat Australia who were world champions – the crowd did a lot for us that day."

The Scarlets v the Ospreys.

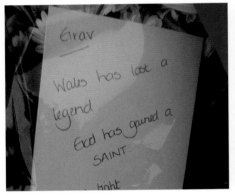

Grav

Wales has lost a

legend.

God has gained a

SAINT

tight

Heaven has gained a
legend that we've lost,
We'll really miss but never
forget you GRAV!!

Cysgu'ch yn dawel!

x x x

WE WILL MISS YOU
RAY
GOD BLESS YOU
FROM
BBC RIGGERS

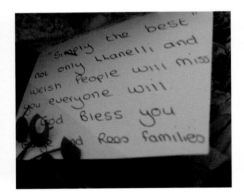

"Simply the best"
not only Llanelli and
Welsh people will miss
you everyone will

God Bless you

and Reos families

November 2007. The death of Ray Gravell provokes an emotional outpouring across Wales and especially at his spiritual home, Stradey Park.

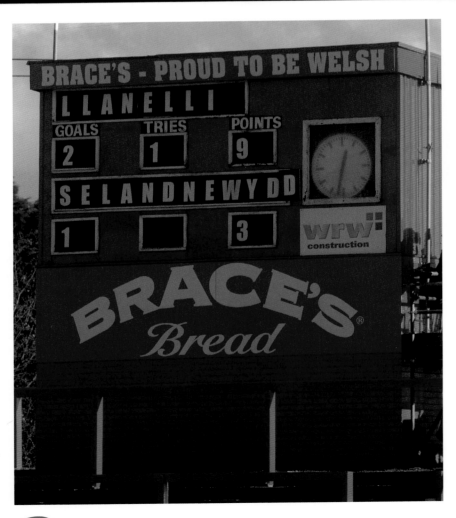

Stradey had never seen anything like the funeral of Ray Gravell. It was attended by thousands, including – clockwise from top left – fellow British Lions, supporters and Wales' First Minister Rhodri Morgan.

There'll be no fireworks
Observation
Scarlets v Leeds

"THE flags are flying at half-mast here at Stradey Park," reporter Gilbert John tells an early evening BBC Radio Wales audience. "And very shortly the fans will gather by their thousands, with a larger than usual crowd expected, because they want to pay tribute to Ray Gravell.

"Tonight's cup match against Leeds is very much taking second place to the tributes although there's no doubt that the Scarlets would regard a victory as their own tribute.

"Despite the tight timescale, officials have managed to revamp the entire early schedule for this game – there'll be no fireworks or blaring music as the players enter; the players will wear black armbands and the Scarlets' shirts will have the word 'Grav' embroidered in gold above their hearts.

"They'll walk rather than run onto the pitch; the children's parade – a regular pre-match feature – will go ahead, and the Scarlets Choir, who had Grav as their president, will sing. The crowd will be asked to join in a minute's applause, not silence – something it's thought that Grav would appreciate.

"Fans are arriving, many simply to look at messages, to read the tributes, to bring their own extra flowers.

"Some of those messages are really, really emotional – there are so many thoughts pinned to a mass of flowers on the gates.

"There are several books of condolence and hundreds of signed special messages. A short time ago a very special floral tribute in the shape of a large rugby ball arrived; it now stands alongside the clubhouse. So many different forms of tributes are emerging; this is a Stradey Park preparing to remember one of its favourite sons."

At the main gates to Stradey Park there are rugby mementoes carrying newly-penned

151

words. A 2000-01 Llanelli RFC shirt in fading scarlet carries the thought: "Diolch am yr atgofion, Ray – John & Donna (Maesteg)."

On the same garment is: "Hwyl fawr, Grav. Rydym yn mynd i gweld eich eisiau yn fawr iawn! Chris & Rebecca (Pontycymer)."

Hastily crafted A4 greetings abound, tied and taped to the gates red iron bars - "Wales has lost a legend … We'll really miss you but never forget you … Simply the best."

Club president and former British Lion Ray Gravell had died two days earlier, on October 31, the 35th anniversary of Stradey Park's most famous day, when Llanelli – with Gravell at centre – beat the All Blacks.

Tributes poured in from around the world and the Scarlets would produce some thrilling rugby to beat Leeds.

Director of rugby Phil Davies would say after the game: "There were a lot of Grav's old teammates here tonight for a special photograph.

"He'd have been proud to see his name on the front of our shirts and he'd have been equally proud of some of the rugby we played tonight.

"He was a proud Scarlet and the longer time goes on over the coming months the more deeply his loss will be felt."

Gravell's funeral at the ground on November 15 would become the one day in the ground's history to match the 9-3 day for emotional power.

Wales' First Minister Rhodri Morgan would speak, the coffin would be carried by British Lions and Grav's young daughters, Manon and Gwenan, would wear rugby shirts celebrating their dad.

A harpist would play, Cor Meibion Llanelli would sing and Burry Port Town Band would play. Throughout, Robin McBryde would carry Grav's weighty Eisteddfod sword.

It would be a day of enormous dignity, respect and celebration. Uplifting anecdotes would be swapped. Grav would have enjoyed the laughter.

Stradey says farewell to Grav. Clockwise, from left, were Robin McBryde, Dafydd Iwan, supporters and Cor Meibion Llanelli.

Tea, cakes and Carwyn

Interview
Peter Rees

PETER Rees sits at his dining table at home above the village of Pembrey.

Born between the wars in the Gwendraeth Valley, he served as Llanelli RFC player, chairman and president across more than four decades. In the amateur era, he had an intricate knowledge of how things worked, of how Stradey Park grew.

He was pivotal to the recruitment of Carwyn James, a coach whose influence has been one of Llanelli rugby's most solid building blocks.

"I became chairman of the club in 1966," says Peter, "and one significant change we made was to head up the playing side with coaches. A gentleman at Stradey told me that something had to be done as we were losing too many matches and weren't playing to our full potential; the boys needed to be fitter. His advice led to us recruiting Tom Hudson, PE director of Swansea University, an Olympic decathlete and a very fit man. Another man contacted me – Ieuan Evans – and he became the coach on the rugby side.

"After a couple of seasons of success, Ieuan moved on because he wanted another challenge, but Barry John's brothers were playing for Llanelli at the time – Alan and Clive – and they told me that Carwyn James was leaving Llandovery College to teach at Trinity College Carmarthen.

"He coached Llandovery College so I rang him and me, my wife and young son went up to Llandovery on a sunny afternoon, went into Carwyn's room, had a cup of tea and a cake and extended an invitation to become Scarlets coach.

"He was delighted and accepted … and within 18 months he'd received a letter from the British Lions asking him to take the 1971 tour to New Zealand. Had we not made that trip for tea and cakes, Carwyn would never have done such great things with Llanelli and the Lions!"

Saracens players applaud their opponents in the Stradey players' tunnel at the end of their EDF Energy Cup game in December 2007. The Scarlets won 36-32.

Peter's rugby started at Gwendraeth Grammar School and he played for Mynydd Mawr Schoolboys. He left school and began working at nearby Cross Hands Colliery where one colleague was shot firer Bert Peel, the grandfather of Stradey scrum-half legend Dwayne. During World War Two, Bert was a trainer at Tumble RFC and his recommendation saw Peter play for the first time at Stradey Park.

Peter says: "Freddie Phillips, an international referee from Pontarddulais, and Dick Edmunds, a senior committee man at Stradey, organised charity games for a local hospital. In around 1943, when I was about 17, I played at Stradey with people like Ted Ward, WTH Davies the outside-half and Trevor Foster. Union and league players could compete together at that stage."

Just before the war ended, Llanelli RFC started playing fixtures again and Peter was in the squad. He says: "When I first played at Stradey, the Tanner Bank and the South Enclosure were just ash. The bank was held back by big baulks of timber brought from the steelworks.

"It's amazing to think that when I played the Wallabies there in 1947 there were about 18,000 in the ground. Hundreds of schoolchildren sat behind the dead ball lines on planks on top of empty brewery casks – the children loved it because they saw the Scarlets and had a half day off school."

At the age of 25 Peter left senior rugby but was back at Stradey in the 1960s.

He says: "One of the most visible things we did in my early days back there was to improve the scoreboard. We only had a feeble wooden structure – just a board with hooks – and it wasn't very high so we

decided to give it more elevation and some modern technology. A nice big clock was presented by a gentleman by the name of W Howells, a jeweller from Tenby. I think it's recently been restored by a clockmaker in Llanelli.

"The new scoreboard was presented to us by WJ Thomas in 1967 – he was an alderman and big at the Trostre tinplate works. The scoreboard was made by the carpentry department at Benjamin Howells, a big timber firm run by WJ Thomas. It was made by local labour and was one of the finest scoreboards of any rugby field. As club chairman I was very proud that we had it and was delighted that WJ Thomas had been kind enough to donate it – the club, as an amateur organisation, couldn't have afforded to pay for such a structure.

"The Town End was a cinder bank at the time so the scoreboard had no concrete plinth or red brick base – it was a scoreboard on stilts. When it eventually came to putting concrete steps there, the board had to be rebuilt with a concrete plinth and with its brick base."

Peter remembers the arrival of Stradey Park's first floodlights. He says: "I was on the committee at the time so it must have been in the early 60s. We managed to acquire some scrap from the Old Castle Works – pylons that had taken overhead gridlines into the works. We dismantled them on site and transported them on a lorry owned by somebody on the committee. At Stradey we got some local boys to lay the concrete and to put the stanchions up. A construction engineer helped put in the bases and the bolts and we had an electricity linesman to assist. We paid very little – as much of the work as possible was voluntary."

As time moved on, it was found that the lights weren't high enough or strong enough so they were eventually replaced. Incidentally, Carwyn James isn't the only Llanelli icon that Peter Rees can claim to have recruited. In the 1960s, as Llanelli RFC chairman, he made a trip to watch a sevens competition in Kidwelly.

He says: "A young scrum-half from Carmarthen's Queen Elizabeth Grammar School impressed me greatly so I invited him to play for our youth side. He did that but as he was coming to the end of his time in the youth he asked me about having a transfer back to Pontyberem where his father had played. I convinced him he had the potential to be a senior Scarlets player, told him to hold his horses and that he'd make it.

"Later on he thanked me for offering that advice … although we did, of course, convert Ray Gravell from being scrum-half to centre."

'You couldn't kick a fart!'

Interview
Terry Davies

YOU might be good enough to tour with the British Lions but you'll never please all the punters all the time. The Stradey Park fans have paid their money, so they'll voice their opinion.

Just ask Terry Davies, a thoroughbred Lion and acknowledged as the world's greatest full-back of his time.

He joined Llanelli in the 1950s and remembers it vividly.

"When I started playing at Stradey Park I remember a huge bank where the North Stand is today," he says in early 2008 at his wonderfully appointed Bynea home.

"The bank would be built up with steelworks slag and it could hold around 5,000 people. They'd stand and cheer you – but you'd also get verbally assaulted from there.

"I remember missing a kick from close to the posts on one occasion and this great big rolling voice rears up and says, 'You couldn't kick a bloody fart!'"

It wasn't just the supporters who expressed an opinion. On Terry's return from the 1959 Lions tour of New Zealand, he was forced to succumb to the steadying influence of the humble Elfed Rees.

Elfed would clean up the dressing room after the players and he'd wait for them, leaning on his brush. He was quite a character – the only one who could speak clearly with a cigarette in his mouth – and he always kept his flat cap just to the side of his head.

Terry, now in his mid-70s, says: "It was so thrilling to play at Stradey Park; after all, the Llanelli rugby team played there – it was the place where Albert Jenkins had played along with all the other great names.

"Albert Jenkins, oh Albert Jenkins – God was second to Albert Jenkins! All the kids knew about Albert Jenkins and his great feats on the rugby field. You knew about Albert Jenkins before you started going to chapel. In fact, no matter how well you played, you'd never play as well as Albert Jenkins had. Albert was a genuine god. I remember returning from that Lions trip – I'd had a hell of a good tour – and I came back to the old bath in the Stradey dressing room.

"It was about 2ft high, made of concrete with about 18ins of water in it. After a game we'd all cram into it – we'd be like sardines.

"I was complaining bitterly about this now, after all we were having crowds of 14,000 and 15,000 and I'd been all over the world in some superb dressing rooms, some with showers. But here we were at Llanelli in this old bath – you'd try to get in first because if a big one jumped in, splashing the water everywhere, there'd be a lot of exuberance, you'd be skidded along the concrete floor of

After the battle – Llanelli RFC players and staff.

the bath and would come out looking like one of those red-arsed baboons.

"I was upset about this facility and I got back to my peg in this very small dressing room and saw that my white shirt had fallen to the floor and someone had left a boot print on it. I was arguing – and suddenly there was a silence and Elfed Rees said to me: 'Hey, good boy – I don't know what you're complaining about, Albert Jenkins bathed in there … and if it was good enough for Albert Jenkins then it's bloody good enough for you!

"I felt tiny – he really shrunk me."

Terry's earliest memories of Stradey Park include sitting through classes at the neighbouring Stradey School during World War Two.

He smiles: "When the air raid hooter went we'd run into the surrounding forest, Stradey Woods. We'd have to hide in there until the all-clear came. There were no air raid shelters – we'd just shelter amongst the trees.

"Every morning we'd hope that the siren would go so we could run into the woods and gather horse chestnuts to eat. You weren't allowed in the woods otherwise but we were devils – we'd slip in there to pick up extra chestnuts.

"Mansel Lewis, who owned the whole thing, would telephone the school and say that boys had been stealing the chestnuts – if you were identified you'd be brought up in front of assembly the next morning to be caned.

"Me and another boy were caught once,

along with a young lad from farming stock – John y Bailey we called him because he was from the Bailey Farm which has since been built on.

"He was a big lad – he'd have to milk the cows in the morning before coming to school, and he'd have to milk them in the evening.

"So one morning the three of us were to be caned for sneaking into the woods, but only two of us turned up in assembly – there was no sign of John. Me and the other lad both had six of the best in front of the whole assembly – not that we'd cry, no way – and then went back to the classroom. Who should be sitting there but John y Bailey. I asked him: 'Why weren't you caned, John?' He said: Oh, my father sent down half a dozen eggs to the teacher!"

BACK ROW: Nathan Thomas, ...
Alix Popham, Phil John, Nathan Br...
MIDDLE ROW: Jon Davies, David ...
Bruce Douglas, Iestyn Thomas, Gav...
FRONT ROW: Liam Davies, Morgan ...
Johnathan Edwards, Ceiron Thomas...

ETS 07/08

Menu, Rhys Priestland, Vernon Cooper, Dafydd Jones, Rob McCusker.
Jones, Matthew Rees, Matthew Watkins.
Jenkins, Dafydd James, Dominic Day, Lou Reed, Adam Eustace, Ben Carter,
Mark Jones, Gavin Evans, Regan King, James Bater, Stephen Jones, Gareth Evans,
Player. NOT PICTURED: Dwayne Peel, Scott MacLeod, Simon Easterby

Stradey Park, 1879-2008